GENTLE HIKES

Minnesota's most scenic North Shore hikes under 3 miles

Ladona Tornabene, Ph.D.
Melanie Morgan
Lisa Vogelsang, Ph.D.

**Adventure Publications, Inc.
Cambridge, MN**

ACKNOWLEDGMENTS

We reserve a very special thank you to the faculty and staff at the University of Minnesota Duluth (UMD), especially the Department of Health, Physical Education and Recreation for its support of this project. Much gratitude to the Dean of the College of Education and Human Service Professions, Vice-chancellor of Academic Administration, UMD's Outdoor Program and Library for further support and assistance.

We would also like to express out appreciation and thankfulness to the employees of the following establishments for their assistance with the completion of this book: All Minnesota North Shore State Parks, especially Gooseberry Falls and Tettegouche; the City of Duluth Parks and Recreation, especially maintenance (a.k.a 'Mr. Walking Encyclopedia'); the Superior Hiking Trail Association (SHTA); Minnesota Department of Natural Resources, Duluth Convention and Visitors Bureau, Wilderness Inquiry, Duluth Seaway Port Authority, U.S. Army Corps of Engineers, Pincushion Mountain Bed and Breakfast, Superior Ridge Resort Motel, The Outpost Resort Motel, Lund's Motel and Cottages, Betty's Cabins, and Solbakken Resort.

We thank the following employees at these establishments for copyright permission to use maps: All Minnesota state parks, Superior Hiking Trail Association, UMD Outdoor Program, City of Duluth Parks and Recreation, Sugarloaf and Two Harbors Area Chamber of Commerce.

Many thanks to Adventure Publications for seeing the need for *Gentle Hikes* and working so closely with us throughout this project.

We would also like to express deep-felt appreciation to our families and friends for all their support, encouragement and piloting. Thank you from the bottom of our 'soles'!

A special thank you to Jabez for a prayer that changed our lives. And last, but certainly not least—The Creator of it all—to whom we give our utmost gratitude. Truly, "The heavens declare the glory of God and the firmament shows and proclaims His handiwork." Ps. 19:1

Please use caution and good sense when participating in outdoor recreational activities. The authors and Adventure Publications, Inc. assume no responsibility for accidents or injuries occurring on the trails, Almost Hikes, waysides, overlooks and picnic areas described in this book.

Learning as much information as you can about the activities and destinations can help prevent accidents and make your recreational experience more enjoyable.

Book design and illustrations by Jonathan Norberg; maps by Anthony Hertzel

DEDICATION

This book is dedicated to the glory of God.
As beautiful as His creation is, it pales in comparison to Him.
It is our hope that you experience both.
Megwich Hchi-Manitou.
Pasa Gweeg!

Happy hiking!
Melanie Morgan
Eph 3:16-17

We'd love to hear what you think about our book-Go to:
www.d.umn.edu/~ltornabe/gh
PLUS - more color photos from the trails!

Healthy TRAILS
Always!
Luevene Tornabe PS 16:11

Happy Trails to you!
Lisa Vogelsang PS 19:1

TABLE OF CONTENTS

INTRODUCTION

Gentle Hikes was created out of a desire to share the outdoors with people of all ability levels.

This book came about after we asked local merchants: "Do you carry a hiking book that focuses on short, relatively easy trails of Minnesota's North Shore?" Very often, their reply was "Well, not exactly..."

It was the first summer of the new millennium. We had friends and family planning a visit and all of them wanted to go hiking! They wanted to experience scenic beauty via the trails, however, some had very limited time here and some had small children. They needed short hikes. Others had certain physical challenges or were totally new to hiking. They needed easier hikes with specific information about the trails such as inclines, steps and surface type.

We began thinking.

One of us authors has a physical limitation and another is temporarily plagued by sports-related injuries. This, combined with the above, made it clear that we needed to locate easier, shorter trails than those most hiking books. Ideas began to flow and *Gentle Hikes* took form.

We have selected the gentlest trails we could locate given the diverse topography of Minnesota's North Shore. Hiking in this area naturally involves inclines, declines, rocks, roots and uneven terrain. We have created a rating system (pg. 18) describing the extent of these elements so that you may choose a trail compatible with your personal abilities. We have also noted which trails meet Universal Design Standards (i.e., trails that meet accessibility standards for persons of all abilities). We have also specified which trails are multi-use, non-motorized paths (i.e., permitting bicyclists and in-line skaters but prohibiting any motorized vehicles with the exception of motorized wheelchairs).

Whereas most of the trails in this book are well-marked and easy to follow, please be aware that we took the liberty to use parts of existing trails to form our own in order to meet the *Gentle Hikes* criteria. When this is the case, it's a good idea to familiarize yourself with the trail description to make sure you stay on course.

Whatever your hiking passion—be it continuous Lake Superior views, dramatic waterfalls, breathtaking vistas, rushing rivers, lush wooded paths or paved scenic trails—this book delivers all of these and much more.

Happy trails and healthy hiking!

Ladona Tornabene, Melanie Morgan, Lisa Vogelsang

Ladona Tornabene, Ph.D., Melanie Morgan, Lisa Vogelsang, Ph.D.

LAYING THE GROUNDWORK

SUGGESTIONS FOR MAKING YOUR HIKES HAPPIER

Since all of our hikes are less than three miles and are on well-marked trails, we list fewer essentials than other resources. Remember to choose trails that are appropriate for your ability and fitness level. Start out slowly and gradually increase your walking speed to a comfortable level, pacing yourself throughout the hike.

Stretch

Stretching before a hike prepares the muscles for activity and stretching after can prevent muscle soreness. Not only does it feel good to stretch, but a flexible muscle is less likely to pull should you move suddenly or accidentally trip.

Rain Gear

We thought we could make it back to the car in time, since it was such a short trail. Lesson learned: always pack a rain jacket! Even though you may start out on a beautiful day, weather conditions can change very quickly on the North Shore. All three of us have been caught in rain storms on trails less than a mile long. Waterproof fabrics that are breathable work best for rain gear.

Clothing Fabric Type

There are many choices in clothing fabric in today's market. Wear something breathable that also dries quickly. Cotton feels great on a hot day, but when it gets wet, it stays wet. Newer nylon and blended synthetics are breathable, help wick perspiration away from the skin and dry much faster than cotton.

Head Coverings

Since your head is obviously closest to the sun, it is important to protect the scalp from the sun's burning rays. Many styles of wide brimmed hats and billed caps can be used to offer head protection and shade the eyes. Whatever your style, choose a hat that offers adequate protection from weather conditions and allows for personal comfort.

Sunscreen

Sunscreens are a necessity in preventing sunburns, wrinkles and reducing the risk of skin cancer. Use a waterproof sunscreen with a minimum of SPF 15. Apply before hiking and re-apply about every hour depending upon perspiration levels. Don't forget sunblock for the lips, nose and ears as well as good quality sunglasses to protect your eyes.

Footwear

The shoes and socks you wear can make the difference between an enjoyable outdoor experience or a hike filled with possible blisters and discomfort. Athletic shoes are great for paved or flat trails without many roots or rocks and are appropriate for trails with a Lighter Side of Gentle rating. Sturdier shoes or hiking boots are a good idea for trails with a Moderate or Rugged Side of Gentle rating. When it comes to shoe or boot fit, don't compromise. Purchase your footwear from a merchant who is knowledgeable about hiking and try on the boots with the type of socks you plan to wear on the trail. After purchasing boots or athletic shoes, it is important to break them in prior to hitting the trails.

Cotton socks are not recommended because they absorb moisture and hold it next to your skin, which may cause blisters or cold feet. Synthetics or other natural fiber socks that are thick or made specifically for hiking are ideal. Some people prefer using a liner sock as well to ensure comfort and reduce the risk of blisters.

The Big Stick

There are several styles of hiking sticks and poles available. Many types have been shown to improve balance and reduce the risk of knee or ankle injury. They are especially useful on declines, inclines and uneven terrain. There are advantages and disadvantages within styles as well as between poles and sticks. If you are considering using a stick or pole, do some homework and talk to local merchants who carry such items. Keep in mind that although most poles are adjustable and some have shock absorption capabilities, their tips can damage tree roots. Hiking sticks are not adjustable and may be heavier to carry, but cause less damage to roots. Whichever you choose, being knowledgeable about proper usage is a must for your safety and the well-being of the environment.

Bug Beaters

Mosquitoes, black flies, gnats, biting flies, ticks, chiggers and sand fleas are all realities to consider when going outdoors. Prevent yourself from being the main course for the bugs' supper by testing which repellent works best for you. Some people swear by a natural soap product called Northwoods Suds. Others like Cactus Juice as a natural remedy. Whether you go natural or traditional, we recommend a product that is healthy for you and the environment. Remember to use repellent on clothing as well as exposed skin. During times of high foliage it is recommended that you wear pants tucked into your socks to prevent tick and other beastie bites.

Water

Drink whether thirsty or not because if you wait until you are thirsty, you are already dehydrated. A good rule of thumb is to bring 8 ounces (1 cup) of water for each 15 minutes of hiking expected. The Superior Hiking Trail Association and other sources recommend allowing 1 hour for every 1.5 to 3 miles of trail covered. Since all of our trails are less than three miles, this means taking a minimum of 32 oz. of water with you (more on a hot day).

Sports drinks are OK, but soft drinks are not recommended, nor are any beverages containing caffeine or alcohol because you will lose more fluid than contained in the drinks. Do not drink water from streams, rivers or lakes unless you have a water purification device to clean the water of bacteria and other impurities.

Snacks

Bring food on hikes lasting longer than an hour. Suggested snack items include dried fruits, crackers, granola, cereal, energy bars and trail mixes. To help keep trails beautiful, pack out anything you take in.

Safety Items

A readily accessible, genuine survival whistle is a necessity even on short hikes. The volume and pitch can scare away unwanted animals or alert others of your position in an emergency. Other items not previously mentioned that we recommend bringing along are personal identification, a small first aid kit, trail maps/descriptions and a small flashlight.

Fun Items

While experiencing the spectacular scenic beauty of these trails, a camera and plenty of film is a North Shore essential! If there's one bug we actually want to bite you, it's the shutterbug! Compact binoculars are also fun to have for identifying birds and butterflies. A small pocket notebook and pen are also nice for recording memories or thoughts.

Daypacks

Backpacks or waist packs are suggested and needed when carrying water or more than one pound of gear. Models with pockets especially for water bottles are convenient. The kind of pack needed depends on the type of hiking you'll be doing, how much gear you plan to carry and its comfort and functionality.

Conclusion

When out on the trail away from modern conveniences, an ounce of prevention is worth more than a pound of cure. Some say it's worth a pound of gold! Implementing the above suggestions may take a little planning and organizing initially, but you'll be glad you brought that pack along.

SCENIC HIGHWAY 61

The North Shore Scenic Drive originates in Duluth and continues 150 miles to the Canadian border. Its primary attraction is impressive landscapes! Rushing rivers, cascading waterfalls, rugged shoreline and cliff face combine with vibrant forests for a dramatic presentation.

The introduction to this All-American Beauty begins as a scenic byway in Duluth and graduates to the prestigious All-American status 19 miles later at Two Harbors, continuing to the Canadian border.

The North Shore Scenic Drive was chosen as an All-American roadway in the year 2000. All-American is the top designation in the National Scenic Byway System, which includes such roadways as the Pacific Coast Highway in California and the Blue Ridge Parkway in North Carolina.

Few roads are awarded the All-American Road status. In fact, according to the National Scenic Byways website: "To receive an All-American Road designation, a road must possess multiple intrinsic qualities that are nationally significant and contain one-of-a-kind features that do not exist elsewhere. The road or highway must also be considered a 'destination unto itself.' That is, the road must provide an exceptional traveling experience so recognized by travelers that they would make a drive along the highway a primary reason for their trip." (http://www.byways.org/travel/scenic_byways.html)

Sit back and enjoy this journey along the North Shore, as this is the highway from which most of our trails, waysides and picnic areas are accessed. Allow plenty of time as this road is not only scenic and beautiful, but a two lane highway (occasional passing lanes) with frequent curves and deer crossings.

TRAILS

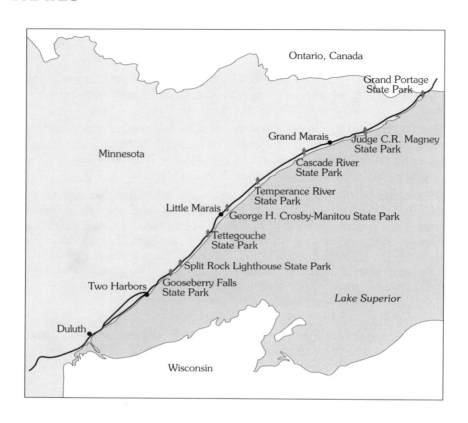

AUTHORS' CORNER

The following groupings of trails are our subjective opinions, but we think you'll be delighted with our selections. Trails are listed in order under each category as they appear on the map starting from Duluth.

Best Lake Superior views:

Best waterfalls:

Best vistas:

Best wooded trails:

Best river views:

Flattest trails:

Paved trails:

*Meets Universal Design Standards

Shortest trails (0.5 mile or less, total length)*:

*Note: Although we did not include our Almost Hikes in the Authors' Corner, we encourage you to browse through their highlights, as most of them fit an above category or two.

TRAIL USAGE INFORMATION

The following is general information pertaining to the majority of trails in this book. For specific questions regarding any particular trail, please contact respective trail headquarters (phone number provided after Trailhead Directions listed on all hikes in this section or see Appendix B).

State Park Trails:

The North Shore is home to eight state parks, which offer numerous hiking trails. Not only have we featured some of the established trails, we have also strung together pathways to create loops or out-and-back treks to provide the most scenic routes we could find within the *Gentle Hikes* criteria (pg. 18).

Certain state parks have multi-use trails (check with individual parks for maps or pick up a copy of *Minnesota's State Parks* by Anne Arthur). Although some parks have designated ATV or snowmobile trails, motorized vehicles are prohibited on all state park hiking trails. Electric wheelchairs are permitted on all state park hiking trails.

Minnesota State Parks offer many amenities. Contact the state parks listed in this book or the Minnesota Department of Natural Resources (1-888-646-6367, www.dnr.state.mn.us).

Superior Hiking Trail (SHT):

Rated as one of the top 10 trails in the country by *Backpacker Magazine*, the 235 mile SHT has received national recognition. This trail is known for its proximity to Lake Superior, spectacular scenery, rugged terrain and steep passageways. We chose the gentlest sections that have entry points, but even so, many sections of this trail earned a Rugged Side of Gentle rating.

The SHT connects to seven North Shore state parks. Although some state parks have designated multi-use trails, please note that motorized vehicles, mountain bikes and horses are prohibited on the Superior Hiking Trail. It is a footpath only trail.

The Superior Hiking Trail Association (SHTA) is a nonprofit, membership driven organization dedicated to the preservation of the Superior Hiking Trail. For more information on SHTA activities or membership, contact (218) 834-2700, www.shta.org or suphike@mr.net.

Note: SHTA lists trail conditions on its website.

Duluth's Lakewalk:

Designed by landscape architect Kent Worley, this very popular paved, multi-use path is Duluth's gateway to Lake Superior. A round trip on the entire Lakewalk is 8 miles, which obviously exceeds our trail length criteria. Therefore, we divided it into five different sections, each with distinct turn-around points.

In each section of the Lakewalk, we showcase its unique attributes, provide entrance access from the closest parking areas and provide various distances, which makes it convenient to hike a single section or string them together for a longer walk.

Although all sections are paved, they do not meet Universal Design Standar
However, two sections are extremely flat (see pg. 180 for more info).

The entire Lakewalk is plowed during snow season; however, access ramps
and boardwalk may be iced over. It is best to call ahead to Duluth Parks and
Recreation at (218) 723-3425 for conditions if visiting in winter.

In addition to its beautiful Lakewalk, Duluth offers many amenities. Call Duluth
Convention and Visitors Bureau, 1-800-438-5884 or www.visitduluth.com.

Bagley Nature Area:

A 50-acre woodland perched atop the University of Minnesota Duluth's campus
offers a great escape right in the heart of a busy venue. There are several paths
that wind around these woodlands. We have pieced together sections to form
three different hikes (including an Almost Hike around Rock Pond, pg. 133).
A spectacular wooded trek in the summer, but especially stunning when
autumn arrives!

For more information on the trails of Bagley, contact UMD's Outdoor Program
at (218) 726-6533 or www.umdoutdoorprogram.org. The Outdoor Programs'
offerings throughout the year include a variety of topics. These programs are
open to the public and campus community.

Note: Bagley borders residential housing, a creek and two roads. Please stay
on the trail and respect others' property.

Pet Policies:

Please pick up after your pet at all times.

State Park Trails: Pets must be on 6 foot leashes. They are not allowed in
park buildings.

Superior Hiking Trail (SHT) sections: Dogs/cats must be on leashes. No pack
animals please.

Duluth's Lakewalk: Pets are welcome on all sections of the Lakewalk; however,
they are not allowed in the Rose Garden (pg.132). Please use sidewalk next to
London Road and follow around to access ramp if you are walking your pet.
Mutt mitts are provided while supplies last.

Bagley Nature Area: No pets allowed.

Trail Closures:

Certain trails in state parks and much of the SHT will be closed during deer
hunting season (typically occurs during the first 3 weeks in November). Please
call ahead to respective trail headquarters or visit their websites (see Appendix B
for a complete listing). The SHT does not recommend hiking on any of their
trails during deer hunting season.

ommodate hikers of all levels, each trail follows a rating system. The rating system is governed by a set of criteria (see below) and offers three levels. Trails range from the Lighter Side of Gentle which includes all paved trails (and more) to the Rugged Side of Gentle which offers more challenge to those who desire it. The Moderate Side of Gentle, as you might expect, falls somewhere in between. All trails are under 3 miles in total length.

Regardless of the rating, each trail will always state the trail surface and width, number of inclines over 10 degrees, steepest and longest incline, safety concerns and all step and bench locations.

Our trail descriptions are very detailed and correspond to the trail in increments of tenths of a mile. We have made every attempt to locate and note trail aspects that may challenge some (e.g., inclines, rocks, roots, steps, etc.) as well as features that may be helpful (e.g., benches, handrailings, paved trails, etc.). With this information, each person can make an informed decision based on his/her abilities as to how far to go on a certain trail or choose another altogether.

Icons:

The following icons represent our trail rating system.

 The Lighter Side of Gentle must meet all of the following criteria (excluding options):

Inclines: 10-12° (or less)
Rock/Root: Minimal (intermittent moderate sections)
Total number of steps encountered throughout the trail: <25
Trail surface: Even (intermittent uneven sections)

 The Moderate Side of Gentle meets ONE or more of the following criteria:

Inclines: 14-16° (or no more than 2 inclines between 18-22°, not exceeding 35' in length)
Rock/Root: Moderate
Total number of steps encountered throughout the trail: <175
Trail surface: Even or uneven

 The Rugged Side of Gentle meets ONE or more of the following criteria:

Inclines: 18-22°
Rock/Root: Moderate to Significant
Total number of steps encountered throughout the trail: <325
Trail surface: Even or uneven, laid log paths possible.

Icons in the Descriptions:

These icons, embedded in the trail description and mileage section for each trail, allow you to quickly see what's ahead on the trail.

 Inclines: Indicates the location of the steepest incline on the trail.

Steps: We note in the description if they ascend/descend, their composition and if they have handrails or not. Non-continuous indicates a brief resting area between sets of steps.

 Benches: Indicates the location of benches on the trail.

 Photo opportunities: On our trails we have chosen places where we thought the views were photo worthy. Some are obvious, others are purely subjective; we think you will be pleased with our suggestions. We have found it to be a great way of preserving and sharing memories for years to come.

Maps:

Provided for each trail, maps show mileage markers that correspond to selected trail descriptions. Not all mileage markers are shown on the maps, only those that will help you locate your position on the trail.

Other Items You'll Find:

 Foot Note:

Information that may be of interest to our readers, including nearby sites to see. These are listed on the specific trails, Almost Hikes, waysides or picnic areas to which they pertain.

 SAYS WHO?

Professional information from research-based articles related to health education issues. These are scattered throughout the book.

An asterisk means that the trail has been given a Gentle Hikes name because no name previously existed or it is part of another trail.

Location • Mileage from Duluth, MN: For consistency, the location of all trails is given as mileage from Duluth, on Highway 61. All state park entrances are on Highway 61 with the exception of George H. Crosby-Manitou State Park. Most sections of the SHT are off various county roads that intersect Highway 61. For Trails, Almost Hikes, Waysides and Picnic Areas in Duluth, directions are given from the SW end of Duluth on Interstate 35.

- **Trail Highlights: Though subjective, we believe that these give an account of the sights you can expect.**

TRAILHEAD DIRECTIONS:

Mile markers are given in tenths of a mile (e.g., 58.5). Actual highway markers are in whole numbers (e.g., 58) and are green with white numbering. Exception: Mile marker 26 in Two Harbors is not posted.

CONTACT:

For more information about the trail, state park or area, get in touch with this organization.

TOTAL TRAIL LENGTH, SURFACE & WIDTH:

Trail length is round trip distance to the nearest tenth of a mile. Trail surface varies from paved, gravel and hardpacked dirt to rock and root. When rock and root are present, they are reported in three categories: minimum, moderate and significant. Please note: Paved trails are not plowed or de-iced during the snow season. One exception is the Lakewalk in Duluth, but call ahead (218-723-3425) if visiting in winter to check conditions.

INCLINES & ALERTS:

Although inclines can be reported as % grade, we chose to use degrees (for conversion table, see Appendix C). The number of inclines exceeding 10° (18% grade), their degree ranges, the steepest incline (its length and location) and the longest incline (exceeding 30') is listed for every trail. Alerts include potential safety hazards or other matters of concern.

TRAILHEAD FACILITIES & FEES:

Unless otherwise noted, facilities are mentioned only if they are at trailhead parking area or on the trail. Fees pertain to parking and entrance. All North Shore state parks require a use permit to enter with the exceptions of Gooseberry Falls Visitor Center and Cascade Falls and Temperance River highway access. Day use or annual permits are available at state park offices.

MILEAGE & DESCRIPTION

0.0 This is your step-by-step description of what you'll encounter on the trail. Not every tenth of a mile is included, usually only those that help you locate your position on the trail or that offer amenities, potential challenges or spectacular views.

Footers help to orientate you throughout the book.

DULUTH TO TWO HARBORS

Bayfront Park • Duluth, MN

- **This wonderfully level paved trail is the Gateway to Duluth's famous waterfront, with commanding views of the Aerial Lift Bridge and an innovative Playfront on the Bayfront designed with little ones in mind!**
- **Home to the annual Bayfront Blues Festival—one of the Midwest's largest outdoor musical venues.**
- **This is a good spot for viewing ships in the harbor.**

TRAILHEAD DIRECTIONS:
Interstate 35 North to Lake Avenue South exit, turn right. Take another right at the first intersection (traffic light) onto Railroad Street and follow for 0.5 mile, past 5th Avenue W to first in-drive for gravel and paved parking lot on lake side of Railroad Street. En route you will have passed the ore carrier *William A. Irvin*, OmniMax and Duluth Entertainment and Convention Center (DECC). Trailhead begins near playground area.

CONTACT:
Duluth Parks and Recreation: (218) 723-3425

TOTAL TRAIL LENGTH, SURFACE & WIDTH:
0.5 mile; asphalt, brick and cement; average 8–15' wide.

INCLINES & ALERTS:
No inclines. This is a multi-use non-motorized path. During special events, other regulations may apply. Trail is not plowed during snow season.

TRAILHEAD FACILITIES & FEES:
Seasonal flush toilets and water fountain. No fees except during Bayfront Blues Festival or other special events.

MILEAGE & DESCRIPTION

0.0 Trailhead begins on asphalt near Playfront, then changes to herringbone pattern brick as you enter Bayfront Festival Park. Directly ahead is the Bayfront stage, nicely framing the Blatnik Bridge, which crosses the harbor into Wisconsin.

0.1 Turn left and begin walking toward the harbor on asphalt path. In 400', you will arrive at an intersection with another part of the Lakewalk entering from the left. Turn right, choosing either asphalt or cement walkway as both run parallel and lead to the same place.

0.2 Stroll out to the deck overlooking the Duluth Harbor. This vantage point provides a commanding view of the Aerial Lift Bridge. Located around the harbor are the Coast Guard installation, Minnesota and Wisconsin points (in the distance) and various loading docks for shipping. Watch for ore boats and also the Vista Fleet, which takes boatloads of sightseers on tour around the harbor.

This area is also a popular kayaking and sailing location as well as the summer home to many species of waterfowl. Geese are especially prevalent here.

0.3 Continue walking the asphalt pathway along the back of the Bayfront stage. As you round the stage area, look toward the city. This vantage point provides an interesting view of the Duluth hillside.

0.4 You will have traveled full-circle as you come to the brick surface again. Turn left to return to parking area.

0.5 Trailhead

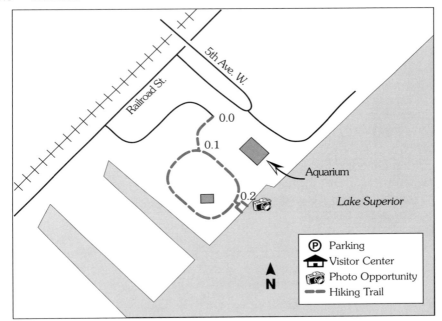

 **Foot Note:**

For information on the Annual Bayfront Blues Festival, contact 715-394-6831 or www.bayfrontblues.com.

Canal wall to Bayfront Festival Park
Duluth, MN

- **Peruse the Lake Superior Maritime Visitor Center, which offers several exhibits and programs on Maritime history.**

- **Striking, close-up views of Duluth's best-known landmark, the Aerial Lift Bridge, which can be raised to a height of 138' in 55 seconds!**

- **Enjoy first-rate views of the shipping canal and Duluth harbor basin throughout this very flat, paved section of the Lakewalk.**

TRAILHEAD DIRECTIONS:
Interstate 35 North to Lake Avenue South exit, turn right. Continue straight onto Canal Park Drive. Trailhead begins at the end of Canal Park Drive in front of Lake Superior Maritime Visitor Center. There are several paved parking lots in this area, but pay close attention to signs as some are reserved, others have hourly limits and many have fees.

CONTACT:
Duluth Parks and Recreation: (218) 723-3425

TOTAL TRAIL LENGTH, SURFACE & WIDTH:
1.2 miles; cement and asphalt; average 8–10' wide; sidewalk sections average 4–5' wide.

INCLINES & ALERTS:
No inclines except gentle ramp access. This is a multi-use non-motorized path. Some sidewalk sections are uneven along Harbor Drive behind the Duluth Entertainment and Convention Center (DECC).

TRAILHEAD FACILITIES & FEES:
Flush toilets and water fountain at Lake Superior Maritime Visitor Center (open year-round; mid-December through mid-March: Friday–Sunday only). Parking fees may apply.

MILEAGE & DESCRIPTION

0.0 Trailhead begins at the doorway to Lake Superior Maritime Visitor Center. This center is operated by the U.S. Army Corps of Engineers and houses some fine exhibits.

At canal wall, when facing the shipping canal, turn right and walk under Duluth's most famous landmark—the Aerial Lift Bridge! The deck of the bridge is not solid, but an open pattern to allow water drainage. This area is also an incredible vantage point for ship watching.

0.3 At intersection, turn left and walk across the Minnesota Slip Bridge. As you look down the waterway, that huge ship is the *William A. Irvin*—a permanent fixture on the Duluth Waterfront. Seasonal tours of this floating museum are available as well as tours of the historic tug *Lake Superior.*

Boats from the Vista Fleet offer fully narrated tours and include Luncheon, Dinner and Moonlight Cruises! A wonderful opportunity to see close-ups of ships and travel under the famous Aerial Lift Bridge. Stop by and visit their office after crossing the slip bridge.

You are now behind the the Duluth Entertainment and Convention Center (DECC) near Harbor Drive facing some of the best harbor basin views around.

0.5 Boardwalk begins. In about 50' there is an informational marker telling about Superior Bay and Duluth Harbor Basin. By now you have probably noticed the Duluth Aquarium to the right. Kids of all ages will enjoy the interactivity and various exhibits.

0.6 The next informational marker tells about the Bayfront Festival Park. The trail continues (see pg. 22 for Bayfront Festival Park); however, to complete this section of the Lakewalk, turn around and retrace path to trailhead.

1.2 Trailhead

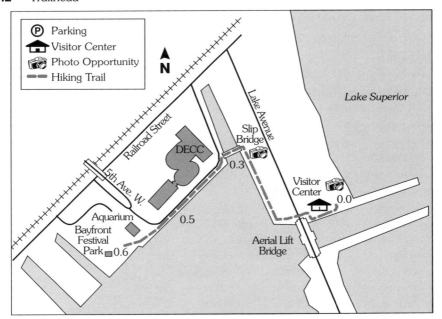

 **Foot Note:**

Seasonal tours are available of the *William A. Irvin*, Flagship of the "Silver Stack" Fleet. (218) 722-7876 or www.decc.org/attractions/irvin.htm.

The Vista Fleet offers fully narrated tours as well as cruises (218) 722-6218.

Canal wall to Fitgers
Duluth, MN

- **One of the absolute flattest sections of the Lakewalk (excluding entrance to Lake Place) to deliver non-stop gorgeous vistas of Lake Superior!**

- **View the Northland Vietnam Veterans' Memorial, Aerial Lift Bridge and shipping industry.**

- **This section is located in the heart of popular Canal Park, which hosts many specialty shops, restaurants and features some magnificent sculptures.**

TRAILHEAD DIRECTIONS:
Interstate 35 North to Lake Avenue South exit, turn right. Continue straight onto Canal Park Drive. Trailhead begins at the end of Canal Park Drive in front of Lake Superior Maritime Visitor Center. There are several paved parking areas in this section, but pay close attention to signs as some are reserved, others have hourly limits and many have fees.

CONTACT:
Duluth Parks and Recreation: (218) 723-3425

TOTAL TRAIL LENGTH, SURFACE & WIDTH:
2.0 miles; cement; boardwalk and blacktop running parallel; average 5–8' wide.

INCLINES & ALERTS:
No inclines. No bikes or in-line skates allowed on boardwalk. Blacktop, which runs parallel to boardwalk is a multi-use non-motorized path. During colder seasons, frost on boardwalk may create slick conditions.

TRAILHEAD FACILITIES & FEES:
Flush toilets and water fountain at Lake Superior Maritime Visitor Center (open year-round; mid-December through mid-March, Friday-Sunday only). Additional seasonal restrooms and water fountain at base of Lake Place steps (near Endion Station). Portable toilets available year-round. Water fountain at Lake Place (seasonal). No fees for trail use, but parking fees may apply.

MILEAGE & DESCRIPTION

0.0 Trailhead begins at canal wall near Lake Superior Maritime Visitor Center in

the heart of Canal Park. When facing the city, to the right is the lighthouse and shipping canal. To the left is a very close look at the Aerial Lift Bridge. This is a fantastic location for viewing ships.

Panoramic vistas of the lake greet you as this trail soon divides into boardwalk and blacktop that parallel each other.

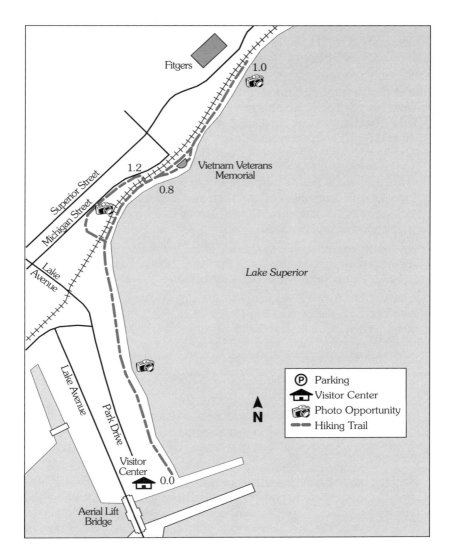

Fitgers

1.0

1.2

0.8

Vietnam Veterans
Memorial

Superior Street

Michigan Street

Lake Avenue

Lake Superior

Lake Avenue

Park Drive

Visitor
Center   0.0

Aerial Lift
Bridge

Ⓟ Parking
🏠 Visitor Center
📷 Photo Opportunity
▬▬ Hiking Trail

▲
N

0.1 To the left are some sights and sounds of Canal Park. Much action typically takes place in Canal Park during the summer. Look up the gravel road; there are usually horse-drawn buggies. This area also periodically features local musicians whose tunes will surely delight the passerby.

Along the boardwalk there are informational markers regarding facts about Lake Superior, the Lakewalk and shipping history. Several strategically placed benches throughout this section of the Lakewalk afford marvelous views of the lake and lighthouse. Pick a favorite spot to sit awhile and watch the ships.

The first marker reveals fascinating facts about Lake Superior. More than 200 rivers flow into the greatest of the great lakes.

The second marker tells about the Lakewalk. As beautiful as the lake is, surprisingly it wasn't always a place of urban development for Duluth. The Duluth Waterfront plan was created in 1986.

0.2 The third informational marker reveals the truth and the fascinating history behind what is referred to simply as The Cribs. A source of mystery and erroneous stories, The Cribs are the remains of a gravel and sand hopper built in 1919. The hopper was constructed so that ships could unload the sand and gravel dredged up for construction without having to enter the harbor and increase congestion. It was also an effort to revive the defunct Outer Harbor Breakwater (which was also built with the intention that ships would be able to unload without entering the harbor) that literally went under in 1872. Lake Superior took down the short-lived commercial enterprise in 1922. All that remains today are timbers and rocks, serving as a hub for aquatic life and the occasional diver's exploration.

0.4 The fourth marker reveals the history of the breakwater ruins. The seemingly insignificant buoy marks the tip of the 1000' strip of submerged rock-filled timber cribs, the ruins of the Outer Harbor Breakwater.

By now you have probably noticed the Image Wall; it extends nearly 600'! It is a mural by Duluth artist Mark Marino composed of several million ceramic tiles depicting chronological scenes of sunken ships. This particular location affords a wonderful view and if you have a panoramic option on your camera, you'll capture an awesome memory.

0.5 Endion Station. This is where the Duluth Convention and Visitor Bureau is located. If you need information on lodging, events or attractions, stop in.

In a few yards find restrooms (seasonal) at the pump station. A portable toilet is open year-round. Observe numerous steps leading up to Lake Place (we recommend continuing on the walk as you will enter Lake Place further along the path).

0.8 Here the boardwalk and blacktop sections of the trail part, but rejoin again shortly. If you choose to visit the Northland Vietnam Veterans' War Memorial, take the boardwalk. This memorial, crafted in the style of the Washington, D.C. Vietnam Memorial, depicts local heroes. The bunker and its strategic placement of sidelights merit a stop at this informational marker.

1.0 The first set of stairs leads to Fitger's Brewery Complex (filled with specialty shops, restaurants and a hotel). The second set of stairs leads to the Portland Malt Shoppe and more specialty shops. Many benches near stair entrance provide exceptional views of the Aerial Lift Bridge and shipping canal as well as the unsurpassed beauty of Superior's coastline.

These stairs signal the end of the boardwalk. The blacktop portion of the Lakewalk continues (see pg. 30 'Rose Garden Park to Fitgers'); however, to complete this section turn around and retrace path to trailhead.

1.2 On the return, as you pass the Vietnam memorial to the left, begin looking to the right across the railroad tracks for a ramp entrance that will bring you to the gardens of Lake Place. After crossing tracks, turn left to enter this three-acre addition with vistas of the lake, Aerial Lift Bridge, shipping lane, lighthouse, pebble beach and rugged rocky shore! Benches abound and you will find a partially enclosed windbreak for wave watching in November.

Lake Place showcases sculptures by various artists and also provides easy access to downtown Duluth.

You can return to the main trail the same way you came or take steps or other ramp leading back down to the boardwalk.

2.0 Trailhead. While you're here, take the "Canal Park Lighthouse Stroll Almost Hike" (pg. 132) to the Lighthouse and save some time to peruse the Lake Superior Maritime Visitor Center, which offers several exhibits and programs on Maritime history.

 Foot Note:

This section of the Lakewalk is used by the American Heart Association for its annual fall HeartWalk, which draws more than 1,000 people (218-727-7297).

 SAYS WHO?

Got 5 minutes?

If you are currently inactive, walking for 5 minutes at a time, 6 times per day, on most days of the week can improve heart health.

Preventive Medicine [5]

Rose Garden to Fitgers
Duluth, MN

- **See the** *Leif Erikson* **Viking Ship that crossed the Atlantic in 1926 using the same route the Vikings traveled on their journey to the new world ten centuries ago!**
- **Commanding views of the Aerial Lift Bridge and, of course, the lake.**
- **Access point to this section of the Lakewalk is home to more than 40,000 roses!**

TRAILHEAD DIRECTIONS:
Interstate 35 North to Lake Avenue South exit, turn left. Turn right at the first traffic light onto Superior Street. At 10th Avenue E, turn right onto London Road (this is where London Road begins and then runs parallel to Superior Street). Drive to paved parking lot on right side of street between S 13th Avenue E and S 14th Avenue E.

CONTACT:
Duluth Parks and Recreation: (218) 723-3425

TOTAL TRAIL LENGTH, SURFACE & WIDTH:
1.4 miles; cobblestone and asphalt; average 8–10' wide.

INCLINES & ALERTS:
No inclines greater than 10°. This section is a multi-use non-motorized path and may be used by in-line skaters and cyclists. Although pets are welcome on the Lakewalk, they are not allowed in the Rose Garden. Please use sidewalk next to London Road and follow around to access ramp if you are walking your pet.

TRAILHEAD FACILITIES & FEES:
Seasonal flush toilets and water fountain available near parking lot. No fees for trail use.

MILEAGE & DESCRIPTION

0.0 Trailhead begins on a bridge (paved, double handrail) located at the far end of the rose garden (see Leif Erikson Rose Garden Almost Hike pg. 132). This bridge is part of an access ramp leading down to the Lakewalk. As you cross the bridge, the Lakewalk and railroad are directly beneath you.

Pause and look left while crossing the bridge for a stunning view of small rock jetties lining the shore of Lake Superior. As you descend the ramp switch-backs, watch for in-line skaters, cyclists and dogs on leashes!

0.1 At the end of ramp, continue straight on asphalt. To the left you will see a now land-based Viking ship. The *Leif Erikson*, a replica of the type of vessel the Vikings used, was built in Korgen, Norway, and sailed from Bergen, Norway, to Duluth, following a North Atlantic route. A project is underway (as of Summer 2001) to "Raise the Roof" over the ship and protect it from the elements. The first intersection brings you to Leif Erikson Park. Turn left toward Viking ship. Two benches are available here, with others scattered along the trail at various intervals. As you continue along this path, look left for 11 uneven steps (stone, no handrail) that lead down to a lovely vista of the lake (guardrail). Another bench provides perfect access to a moment of tranquility. Back on the trail, the open-air amphitheater will be to your left. Take the path straight ahead to regain access to the main Lakewalk, then turn left.

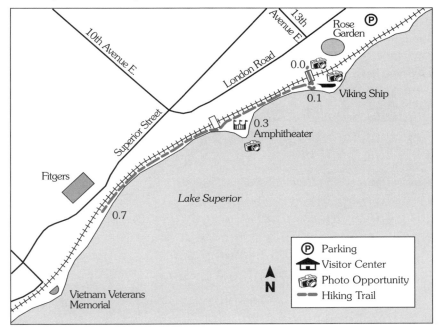

0.3
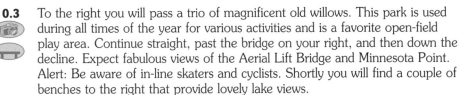
To the right you will pass a trio of magnificent old willows. This park is used during all times of the year for various activities and is a favorite open-field play area. Continue straight, past the bridge on your right, and then down the decline. Expect fabulous views of the Aerial Lift Bridge and Minnesota Point. Alert: Be aware of in-line skaters and cyclists. Shortly you will find a couple of benches to the right that provide lovely lake views.

0.5
Find two more benches to the left with a commanding view of Lake Superior. They also provide a nice view of the Aerial Lift Bridge and shipping canal.

0.7
This portion of the Lakewalk brings you to the entrance of Newfound Beach. A gentle gravel decline leads to its pebbled shore. A great place for skipping stones for the young and young at heart! The set of steps to the right leads to Portland Malt Shoppe. Cool down with a frozen treat before heading back to the trailhead. Or if you prefer a hot version, it's just another 200' to the second set of steps leading up to Fitgers Complex where you can get a great

espresso or cappuccino from the coffee shop. Also, many specialty shops and restaurants are housed in the Complex.

The Lakewalk continues into Canal Park ('Canal Wall to Fitgers' pg. 26); however to complete this section, turn around and retrace path to trailhead.

1.4   Trailhead.

 Foot Note:

The amphitheater hosts the Lake Superior Shakespeare Festival. For more information on this and other events in the Park, call 1-800-438-5884 or www.visitduluth.com.

Historical information about Leif Erikson Park and Duluth derived from Aubut, S.T. and Norton, M.C. (2001) *Images of America Duluth, Minnesota*, Chicago: Arcadia.

 SAYS WHO?

Want to decrease your chances of getting a stroke? Get in stride!

Walking briskly for about 30 minutes a day can reduce the risk of stroke by about 30%.

Journal of the American Medical Association [7]

Aerial Lift Bridge (see pg. 24). Photo by Ladona Tornabene

Rose Garden to Water Street
Duluth, MN

- **Access point to this section of the Lakewalk is home to more than 40,000 roses!**
- **Experience some of Superior's most scenic rugged shoreline—especially beautiful when waves are crashing.**

TRAILHEAD DIRECTIONS:
Interstate 35 North to Lake Avenue South exit, turn left. Turn right at the first traffic light onto Superior Street. At 10th Avenue E, turn right onto London Road (this is where London Road begins and then runs parallel to Superior Street). Drive to paved parking lot on right side of street between S 13th Avenue E and S 14th Avenue E.

CONTACT:
Duluth Parks and Recreation: (218) 723-3425

TOTAL TRAIL LENGTH, SURFACE & WIDTH:
1.8 miles; cobblestone and asphalt; average 8–10' wide.

INCLINES & ALERTS:
No inclines greater than 10°. This section is a multi-use non-motorized path. Although pets are welcome on the Lakewalk, they are not allowed in the Rose Garden. Please use sidewalk next to London Road and follow around to access ramp if you are walking your pet. Street crossing is necessary if you continue through optional interrupted section of the Lakewalk.

TRAILHEAD FACILITIES & FEES:
Seasonal flush toilets and water fountain available near parking lot. Portable toilet available year-round at end of Lakewalk East. No fees for trail use.

MILEAGE & DESCRIPTION

0.0 Trailhead begins on a bridge (paved, double handrail) located at the far end of the rose garden (see Leif Erikson Rose Garden Almost Hike pg. 132). This bridge is part of an access ramp leading down to the Lakewalk. As you cross the bridge, the Lakewalk and railroad are directly beneath you.

Pause and look left while crossing the bridge for a stunning view of small rock jetties lining the shore of Lake Superior. As you descend the ramp switchbacks, watch for in-line skaters, cyclists and dogs on leashes!

0.1 At end of ramp, turn right and follow Lakewalk as you head northeast along Duluth's rugged yet beautiful lakeshore.

0.2 To the left is a picnic table set amid summer wildflowers. Optional spur trail (gravel and hardpacked dirt) to the right leads through a wooded area and offers a respite from the main path. It leads down to the lake and onto rocky outcrops, then rejoins the Lakewalk via 6 uneven steps (stone, no handrail). A couple of benches allow you to pause and enjoy the moment.

0.3 This section has many picnic tables and park benches that have been placed for your enjoyment. Impressive views of the Aerial Lift Bridge and Lake Superior's rugged shore abound.

Note: Building on the left is not a restroom, even though it looks like one from a distance. It is a sewer lift station.

0.6 By now you have noticed the huge structure to the left. It is an overpass with paved switchbacks that leads to 17th Avenue E.

0.9 The "Lakewalk East" sign signals an interruption in the Lakewalk. It does continue (see pg. 36 'London Road to Water Street') but you'll need to walk along the sidewalk of Water Street for another 0.2 mile and cross S 23rd Avenue E to locate it. However, to complete this section, turn around and retrace path to trailhead.

1.8 Trailhead

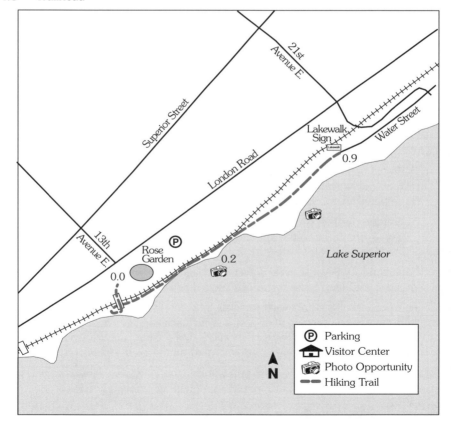

London Road to Water Street
Duluth, MN • *Gentle Hikes name

- **The road less traveled by describes this section of the Lakewalk, which features a more rugged shoreline, including small cliff views.**

- **More trees, fewer lake views; combination of elements give a remote feeling to a city hike.**

TRAILHEAD DIRECTIONS:

Interstate 35 North to end; at split veer left (do not follow North Shore). Cross London Road and begin up 26th Avenue E turning right onto Alexander Street (first street after gas station). Follow to paved parking area.

CONTACT:

Duluth Parks and Recreation: (218) 723-3425

TOTAL TRAIL LENGTH, SURFACE & WIDTH:

1.6 miles; asphalt; average 6–8' wide.

INCLINES & ALERTS:

No inclines greater than 10°. This section is a multi-use non-motorized path. Trail crosses railroad tracks after leaving parking lot. Street crossing is necessary if you continue through optional interrupted section of the Lakewalk.

TRAILHEAD FACILITIES & FEES:

No facilities available. No fees for trail use.

MILEAGE & DESCRIPTION

0.0 Trailhead begins at bike route sign, on a gradual decline. Soon you will cross railroad tracks and continue parallel to them through a tunnel (there is a big fence between you and the tracks).

0.2 At first intersection is a stop sign. Watch for bicycles and in-line skaters. The Lakewalk continues to the left and to the right. For now, turn right (at mile 1.0 we will take you to the left).

0.3 Look carefully because tucked away to the left is a bench that faces an impressive view of Lake Superior's rugged coastline.

0.4 This portion of the Lakewalk parallels Interstate 35. The huge structure to your right is an overpass with paved switchbacks and provides access across I-35 to restaurants, lodging and specialty shops. Here's your opportunity to grab a sandwich and enjoy lakeview dining on the picnic tables provided.

As you walk along this section, you will lose the lake view. However, you will gain views of spruce, aspen, maple, mountain ash, pine and willow.

0.6 This brings you to the intersection of S 23rd Avenue E and Water Street, which signals an interruption in the Lakewalk. It does continue (see pg. 34 'Rose Garden to Water Street') but you'll need to cross S 23rd Avenue E and walk along Water Street for another 0.2 mile toward 'Lakewalk East' sign to locate it. To complete this section, turn around and retrace path toward the first intersection at the stop sign.

1.0 Back at that first intersection, do not return to the parking lot but continue straight (this would have been a left at mile 0.2). Soon you'll travel through a nice stand of aspen, then experience some surprisingly rugged beauty.

1.2 Look at the cliff views here. They aren't the tallest, but are a sweet surprise right in the middle of the city. They are especially striking when waves are crashing.

London Road sidewalk signals the end. Turn around and retrace path back to stop sign at intersection.

1.4 Stop sign at intersection. Turn right and head back to parking area.

1.6 Trailhead

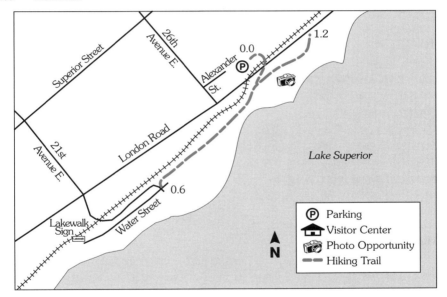

 SAYS WHO?

"Exercise can reduce the risk of heart disease more effectively than most drugs."

Circulation [18]

University of Minnesota Duluth • Duluth, MN

- **Features a panoramic view of Duluth harbor, Park Point, portions of Wisconsin, Lake Superior, UMD campus and some of Duluth's wooded highlands.**
- **Travels through a forest rich in maple.**

TRAILHEAD DIRECTIONS:

Interstate 35 North to exit 258 (watch for sign indicating University of Minnesota Duluth), turn left at the end of exit ramp. Continue up 21st Avenue East until it ends at Woodland. Turn right and follow for 0.9 mile to St. Marie Street (traffic light and gas stations at corner). Turn left and follow for 0.5 mile to one block beyond Montrose Avenue. Turn right into paved parking lot (watch for sign indicating Bagley Nature Area). Note: If parking during September to May, see Alert section below.

CONTACT:

UMD Outdoor Program: (218) 726-6533

TOTAL TRAIL LENGTH, SURFACE & WIDTH:

0.9 mile; grass and mulched trail; average 5–6' wide. Minimal rock and root.

INCLINES & ALERTS:

There are two inclines of 12° each. The longest is 40' at 0.3 mile. Parking is limited to the few meters in this lot near trailhead during September through May. Additional parking in pay lot located to the right on University Drive.

TRAILHEAD FACILITIES & FEES:

No facilities available. From September–May, there is a fee for parking (unless you are fortunate enough to find street parking that is not in a residential zone).

MILEAGE & DESCRIPTION

0.0 Trailhead begins near metered parking area and kiosk map display. Enter trail by yellow gate and immediately experience the tranquility of Rock Pond as you travel through open area amid ash, birch and maple. At first intersection, turn left, then turn right at next intersection.

0.1 This section brings you into a rather large open area with trails heading off in three directions. Take the middle trail. At the next intersection, continue straight.

0.3 In this section you will encounter two areas of incline with the first being the steepest (12° for 40'). At the first intersection, turn right and continue up the trail. Further along, turn left to the gravel path; turn left again and up the dirt and gravel road.

0.5 You will arrive at the top of Rock Hill where you will find a small spur leading to an observation deck (guardrails). From this vantage point you can see a panorama of Duluth harbor, Park Point, Wisconsin, Lake Superior and the UMD campus. If you are fortunate enough to visit in the fall, the trees may be ablaze with color.

Retrace your path back down the hill and turn right into the woods at the previous gravel path. Turn right on mulched trail, then right again in about 50'. At the next intersection, turn right once more. You will come to an area of decline (14° for 50').

0.7   At the next intersection, turn left. This brings you into a nice stand of maple and birch. Soon you will come to another intersection; turn left and encounter another area of decline (14° for 60'). Turn right at the next intersection.

0.8   This section returns you to the clearing. Turn right, then right again at the next intersection. Next you will come to another clearing. At Y in trail, take path to the left. It will bring you to the parking area. (Note: Hike does not loop completely around pond).

0.9   Parking area and trailhead.

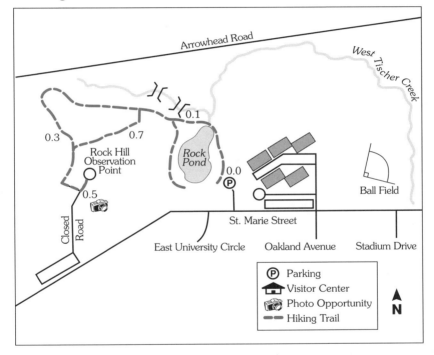

![rose] **Foot Note:**

This trail overlooks UMD campus, which offers a variety of undergraduate and graduate degrees (218-726-8000 or www.d.umn.edu).

University of Minnesota Duluth • Duluth, MN • *Gentle Hikes name

- **One of the few trails to feature significant numbers of oak trees.**
- **Travels through a forest rich in maple.**

TRAILHEAD DIRECTIONS:
Interstate 35 North to exit 258 (watch for sign indicating University of Minnesota Duluth), turn left at the end of exit ramp. Continue up 21st Avenue East until it ends at Woodland. Turn right and follow for 0.9 mile to St. Marie Street (traffic light and gas stations at corner). Turn left and follow for 0.5 mile to one block beyond Montrose Avenue. Turn right into paved parking lot (watch for sign indicating Bagley Nature Area). Note: If parking during September to May, see Alert section below.

CONTACT:
UMD Outdoor Program: (218) 726-6533

TOTAL TRAIL LENGTH, SURFACE & WIDTH:
0.8 mile; grass and mulched trail; average 5' wide.

INCLINES & ALERTS:
There is one incline of 16° for 25' at 0.4 mile. Parking is limited to the few meters in this lot near trailhead during September through May. Additional parking in pay lot located to the right on University Drive.

TRAILHEAD FACILITIES & FEES:
No facilities available. From September–May, there is a fee for parking (unless you are fortunate enough to find street parking that is not in a residential zone).

MILEAGE & DESCRIPTION

0.0   Trailhead begins near metered parking area and kiosk map display. Enter trail by yellow gate and immediately experience the tranquility of Rock Pond as you travel through open area amid ash, birch and maple. At intersection, turn right and proceed up slight incline.

0.1   To the right of the next intersection, you will see the volleyball area. Continue straight here and at the following two intersections.

0.3   At next intersection, turn left (if you arrive at the baseball field, you've gone too far).

0.4   You will now be walking along the Tischer Creek to your right. Beyond that, through the trees, is Arrowhead Road. You will encounter the area of steepest incline (16° for 25') in this section.

0.5   This portion of the trail brings you to two Y-type intersections: turn right at the first, then left at the second.

0.7 Now you've returned to the main trail where you previously noticed the volleyball court. Turn right at this intersection, then left at the next, which will bring you back to the beginning of the trail.

0.8 Trailhead

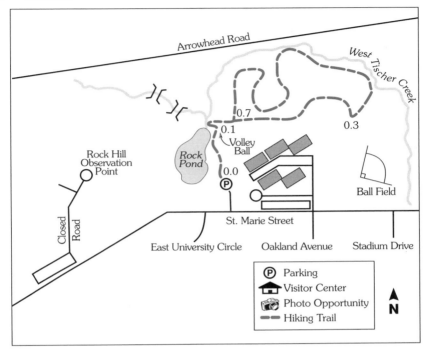

 **Foot Note:**

"The real classroom is outside...get into it!" This quote is from UMD's Outdoor Program, which offers a variety of year-round programs (218-726-6533 or www.umdoutdoorprogram.org).

University of Minnesota Duluth • Duluth, MN • *Gentle Hikes name

- **Awesome wooded hike with quaint pond and small bridges, right on the University of Minnesota Duluth's campus.**
- **Especially gorgeous in fall—exuberant colors!**
- **Forest abounds with groves of maple.**

TRAILHEAD DIRECTIONS:

Interstate 35 North to exit 258 (watch for sign indicating University of Minnesota Duluth), turn left at the end of exit ramp. Continue up 21st Avenue East until it ends at Woodland. Turn right and follow for 0.9 mile to St. Marie Street (traffic light and gas stations at corner). Turn left and follow for 0.5 mile to one block beyond Montrose Avenue. Turn right into paved parking lot (watch for sign indicating Bagley Nature Area). Note: If parking during September to May, see Alert section below.

CONTACT:

UMD Outdoor Program: (218) 726-6533

TOTAL TRAIL LENGTH, SURFACE & WIDTH:

0.4 mile; grass and mulched surface; average 5–6' wide. Minimal rock and root.

INCLINES & ALERTS:

No inclines greater than 10°. Parking is limited to the few meters in this lot near trailhead during September through May. Additional parking in pay lot located to the right on University Drive.

TRAILHEAD FACILITIES & FEES:

No facilities available. From September–May, there is a fee for parking (unless you are fortunate enough to find street parking that is not in a residential zone).

MILEAGE & DESCRIPTION

0.0   Trailhead begins near metered parking area and kiosk map display. Enter trail by yellow gate and immediately experience the tranquility of Rock Pond as you travel through open area amid ash, birch and maple. At first intersection turn left; at next intersection turn right.

0.1   This leads you through stands of maple and into an open area with trails heading off in three directions. Take the one furthest right and into the woods through more maple. Very soon you will cross a bridge (wood, double handrail). At the next intersection, continue straight on main path.

0.2   Soon you will find a bench. Take a few minutes to enjoy the beauty of your surroundings amid maple, aspen, birch and fern. Cross bridge (wood, double handrail).

0.3   The next intersection gives you several directional choices, but for this hike turn left. It will bring you back to the open area you found earlier. Take the trail to your right and follow to Rock Pond. Turn right and follow around the pond through a stand of pine.

0.4 This section brings you to another clearing. At Y in trail, take path to the left. It will bring you to the parking area. (Note: Hike does not loop completely around pond).

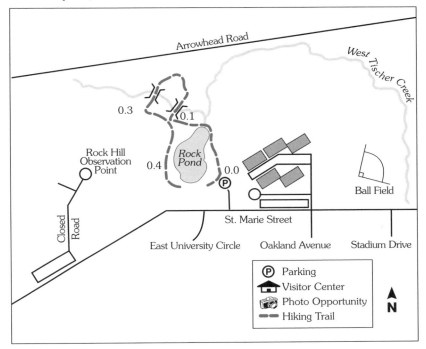

 **Foot Note:**

Bagley consists of 50 acres and is located on the UMD campus. It is an area of unique study and features flora of unusual diversity.

Congdon Park • Duluth, MN

- **A must-see for waterfall enthusiasts! What these lack in power they deliver in delicate beauty.**

- **Allow time to explore the many short spur trails that deliver virtually non-stop action of cascades and waterfalls!**

- **This hike gives a definite North Shore feel—right in the heart of Duluth.**

TRAILHEAD DIRECTIONS:

Interstate 35 North to end. Cross London Road and begin up 26th Avenue E and turn right onto Superior Street. Follow to 32nd Avenue E. Paved parking is available on Superior Street June 16–August 30. Otherwise, during the school year (September 1–June 15, 8–4 p.m. Monday–Friday) this becomes a resident permit parking zone only.

CONTACT:

Duluth Parks and Recreation: (218) 723-3425

TOTAL TRAIL LENGTH, SURFACE & WIDTH:

1.3 miles; gravel and hardpacked dirt; average 2–4' wide. Moderate rock and root.

INCLINES & ALERTS:

There are two inclines at 14°. Steepest incline is 14° for 25' at 0.1 mile. Wet areas possible. Some steep cliffs in river gorge areas.

TRAILHEAD FACILITIES & FEES:

No facilities available. No fees for trail use.

MILEAGE & DESCRIPTION

0.0 Trailhead begins just past Congdon Park Drive near bridge abutment on the hill side (as opposed to the lake side) of Superior Street near sign for Congdon Park. Begin downhill side of trail. Descend 28 uneven steps (stone, no handrail). At bottom of steps, turn left. Enjoy the feeling of remoteness and tranquility as you journey through a lovely wooded area of maple, fir, cedar and willow.

This section of trail has two bridges with steps (all wood, double handrail) leading up to them and steps leading back down from them. The first one has 7 steps leading up, then 5 back down. The second bridge has 6 leading up, then 6 back down. While crossing Tischer Creek, pause to take in the views as they frame some great photo ops!

About 50' beyond the second bridge is an intersection: either direction brings you to the same place. As you walk through a deep gorge, look right for a delightful waterfall over the rhyolite cliff. When conditions are optimal, its appearance is simply striking.

Tall pines have now joined the park ecosystem.

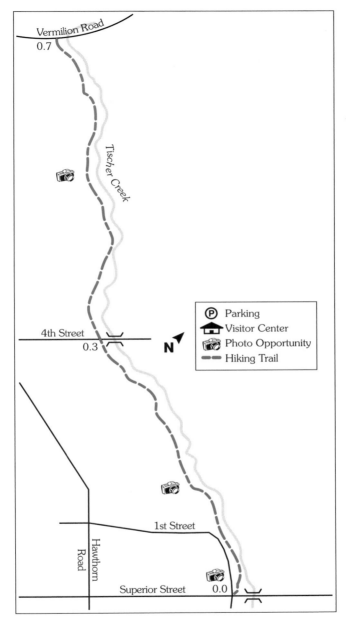

Vermilion Road

0.7

Tischer Creek

4th Street

0.3

N

P Parking
Visitor Center
Photo Opportunity
Hiking Trail

1st Street

Hawthorn Road

Superior Street   0.0

0.1 This section contains several sets of steps and bridges. Use caution if surfaces are wet. Ascend 8 uneven steps (stone, double handrail). Ascend 10 steps, cross bridge, then ascend 10 more steps (all wood, double handrail). Pause to watch Tischer Creek beneath you as it cascades down the rhyolite. A 10' concrete walk leads to 10 additional steps up (wood, double handrail). You will cross another bridge over the creek, then descend three steps (concrete, double handrail).

A significantly rocky (rhyolite) area on the trail precedes your ascent of 45 uneven steps (stone, no handrail, non-continuous). The area of steepest incline (14° for 25') will be found in a rocky, rooted section, followed by a step-like rooted incline.

At next intersection, turn right. Use caution at cliff edge. You will be walking along a ridge overlooking the Tischer Creek gorge. Further down the trail, ascend 4 more uneven steps (stone, no handrail).

0.2 At the next intersection, turn left then right to main trail. A few feet further you will find a newer bench. The trail surface has changed to gravel and hard-packed dirt. In approximately 200', a spur to the right leads to a lovely falls view. Alert: Though beautiful, this area is rocky and has steep dropoffs with no guardrails. From this area of rock, another trail leads down to the river via a set of steep steps with vertical rise exceeding 12". We do not recommend this as there are much easier access areas elsewhere on the trail.

Return to the main trail. As you continue, an incline precedes an intersection; continue straight.

0.3 You will come to a Y in the trail; turn left, then right on asphalt surface. This section of the trail is somewhat uneven; it will bring you to 4th Street. Use caution when crossing the street, then re-enter at sign indicating "Congdon Park 1.5 mile hiking trail" on a 4' wide gravel and hardpacked dirt surface. Notice that oak trees have joined the Congdon Park ecosystem. The trail will take on more rock due to erosion.

The most challenging part of the remainder of this trail will be deciding which spur to take to the river. Our opinion? Allow enough time to take them all! Explore at your leisure as these short detours are really grand tours leading to exquisite views of rumbling cascades, delicate waterfalls and lazy reflection pools. Photo ops abound!

0.5 Especially lovely views of waterfalls and boulders along the creek.

0.7 This brings you to the base of 10 steps (stone, no handrail) that will lead to the intersection of Vermilion Road and E St. Marie. At this point, turn around and begin retracing path toward trailhead.

1.0 After crossing 4th Street., return to the asphalt trail.

1.2 Stay on the asphalt path until you come to the intersection of Congdon Park Drive and E 1st Street. Turn left and find the gravel path that runs along the top of the ridge above the creek. This will return you to the trailhead.

1.3 Trailhead

Gooseberry Falls (see pg. 56). Photo by Ladona Tornabene

 Foot Note:

Duluth, Minnesota has been named one of America's Great Outside Towns by *Outside Magazine*. (September 2001 issue)

 SAYS WHO?

Want to get smart? Work out the heart!

Walking improves the functioning of the brain.

American Fitness [23]

LESTER PARK TRAIL

Lester Park • Duluth, MN

- **A lovely wooded hike along Lester River and Amity Creek which range from gentle rumbles to roaring rapids!**
- **A quaint gazebo offers views of small waterfalls; one of the cobblestone bridges from the historic Seven Bridges Road can be seen nearby.**
- **Nice playground and picnic area at the beginning of this trail.**

TRAILHEAD DIRECTIONS:

Interstate 35 North to end; at split veer left (do not follow North Shore). Cross London Road and begin up 26th Avenue E turning right onto Superior Street. At intersection of Superior Street and Lester River Road (approximately 61st Avenue E), turn left onto Lester River Road. Paved parking lot is immediately on the left.

CONTACT:

Duluth Parks and Recreation: (218) 723-3425

TOTAL TRAIL LENGTH, SURFACE & WIDTH:

0.8 mile; cement, hardpacked dirt and gravel; average 3–4' wide. Minimum rock and root.

INCLINES & ALERTS:

No inclines greater than 10°. Steep cliffs; some have rails. Wooden bridges can be very slippery when wet.

TRAILHEAD FACILITIES & FEES:

Flush toilets (seasonal, not wheelchair accessible as of 12/01), covered picnic tables, playground. No fees for trail use.

MILEAGE & DESCRIPTION

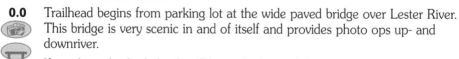

0.0   Trailhead begins from parking lot at the wide paved bridge over Lester River. This bridge is very scenic in and of itself and provides photo ops up- and downriver.

If you brought the kids, they'll love what's next! A nice playground for them and a couple of benches for you with lots of greenspace to enjoy. All of this and picnic tables too (including an open-sided shelter) spell great family fun.

Continue to follow sidewalk around playground area until it ends. Turn right onto 6' wide gravel path and head toward bridge (wood, double handrail). Pause and take in the view of Amity Creek. Immediately after crossing bridge turn right at trail intersection (do not continue up steps).

0.1   As you enter the wooded section of this trail, you'll cross another bridge (wood, handrail). You will also be traveling on a ridge overlooking the waters.

0.2   Cross another bridge (wood, handrail). At Y, continue straight following river.

0.3   At next Y, veer left; stay on trail and head toward gazebo.

0.4 Gazebo and bench. After enjoying the views, cross over the bridge (cobblestone, double handrail). Look to the left for historical Seven Bridges Road. At trail intersection, turn right.

0.5 As you cross yet another bridge (wood, handrails), look between the trees for a waterfall view. Depending on conditions, this one can be striking!

0.6 Trail merges with another hiking trail from left. Continue straight on wide path. Follow trail to playground, then on to parking lot.

0.8 Trailhead

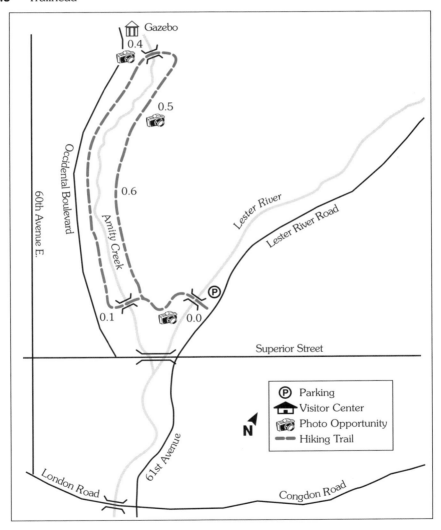

SHT Section: Knife River to Lake County Road 102
On Scenic Highway 61, 13 miles from Duluth

- **This is a lovely hike along Knife River on a beautifully wooded path and is especially scenic after leaves have fallen.**
- **Knife River is a designated trout stream.**

TRAILHEAD DIRECTIONS:
Travel northeast from Duluth on London Road until it ends at a split (options: Expressway or Scenic Highway 61). Veer right onto Scenic Highway 61. There are no mile markers, but you will be going toward the town of Knife River. Travel 13 miles to parking area located on left side just before Knife River bridge and Marina Road, opposite Depot Campground. Look for sign indicating Superior Hiking Trail (SHT) parking.

CONTACT:
Superior Hiking Trail: (218) 834-2700

TOTAL TRAIL LENGTH, SURFACE & WIDTH:
0.8 mile; gravel, grass and hardpacked dirt; average 2–4' wide. Minimal root. Moderate rock for one small section only.

INCLINES & ALERTS:
No inclines greater than 10°. Some trail erosion along riverbank as well as runoff areas and uneven surfaces. May have standing water; no footbridge. Trail closes for deer hunting season (typically the first three weeks of November).

TRAILHEAD FACILITIES & FEES:
No facilities available. No fees for trail use.

MILEAGE & DESCRIPTION

0.0 Trailhead begins in parking area at sign indicating First Falls and Expressway. Enter a mixed forest as you hike along Knife River. This is especially scenic after leaves have fallen. Alert: Watch for trail erosion and runoff areas along riverbank. At first intersection, continue straight. Soon you will encounter a lookout point with great views downriver. At next two intersections, veer right, following the river.

Further on, you will see the trail split for approximately 20', then reconnect. Immediately after this a spur trail to the right takes you to the river's edge. However, there were several downed trees and numerous rocks. You will find it easier to stay on the main trail.

0.3 At next Y, veer right staying close to the river. Look for small SHT sign on tree. Notice that pine have joined the forest and cedars begin lining the riverbank. This is the only section in which you will find moderate rock.

Look across the river to see sets of wooden stairs. These can be accessed from the Knife River Wayside (pg. 148).

You may notice a cable strung across the river and a sign stating "Fish Sanctuary -No fishing between cables." You are nearing the falls area. At next intersection, turn right onto wide, packed dirt trail.

0.4 You have reached the First Falls. The falls are small yet picturesque as ribbons of water tumble gently toward the river.

Turn around and re-enter the wooded area following the 8' wide trail. This direction creates a nice loop hike. Continue to follow the wide path until reaching the gate near the parking area (spurs to the right lead to private property; please respect boundaries). Turn left and walk toward the trailhead. Note 2-sided info board about Knife River Stewardship Project and interesting fish facts.

0.8 Trailhead.

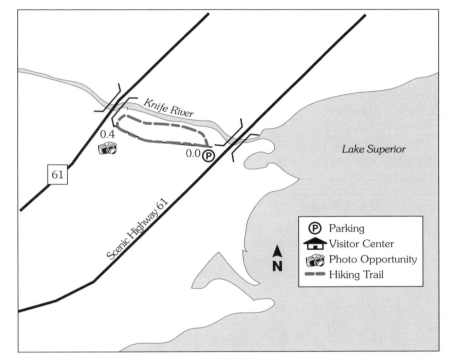

Lighthouse Loop
Two Harbors, MN • Off Highway 61, 26 miles from Duluth

- **Breathtaking, expansive views of Lake Superior!**
- **Original Two Harbors Lighthouse–the oldest operating lighthouse in Minnesota.**

TRAILHEAD DIRECTIONS:
Highway 61 at mile marker 26 (Note: you will not find actual mile marker—use odometer reading from marker 25), turn right onto Waterfront Drive (corner of Dairy Queen and Blackwoods Restaurant) and follow for 0.5 mile to South Avenue. Turn left and follow for 0.3 mile to 3rd Street; turn right and follow for 0.2 mile to paved parking area.

CONTACT:
Two Harbors Area Chamber of Commerce: 1-800-777-7384

TOTAL TRAIL LENGTH, SURFACE & WIDTH:
0.5 mile; paved, gravel; average 6–8' wide. Minimal rock and root.

INCLINES & ALERTS:
There are two inclines at 12°. Steepest and longest is 12° for 40' at 0.1 mile. Trail is not a complete loop but finishes at far end of parking area.

TRAILHEAD FACILITIES & FEES:
Portable toilets (seasonal) in parking lot. No fees for trail use.

MILEAGE & DESCRIPTION

0.0 Trailhead begins in parking area nearest in-drive on boulder-lined asphalt path (there is no sign for trailhead). In 75', come to intersection with 6' wide gravel path; turn right. The forest begins with alder thicket yielding to aspen, then fairly large birch culminating with a stand of cedars. There are several spur trails in this area; stay on main path.

0.1 Area of steepest incline (12° for 40'). Atop this hill sits the first of many
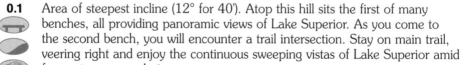 benches, all providing panoramic views of Lake Superior. As you come to the second bench, you will encounter a trail intersection. Stay on main trail, veering right and enjoy the continuous sweeping vistas of Lake Superior amid fragrant spruce and pine.

Stroll out to one of the benches and watch the gulls floating lazily on the water. Ships that trade within the Great Lakes only are called Lakers in Great Lakes or Seaway slang, while ships that pass through the St. Lawrence Seaway to the Atlantic Ocean and beyond are called Salties.

The relatively level spur trails and fairly flat rock provide ample opportunity for coastline exploration. Notice the pools of water held captive in rocky pockets. These make wonderful photos!

0.3 Look right to see the original Two Harbors Lighthouse which first shone on Lake Superior in 1892 and continues today making it the oldest operating lighthouse in Minnesota. Beside it rests the restored pilot house recovered from the ore boat *Frontenac*.

0.5 As you pass under the Spirit of Two Harbors archway, you'll be at the opposite end of the parking area from the trailhead. While you're here, take time to explore the Breakwater Lighthouse Point Stroll (see pg. 135).

Trailhead.

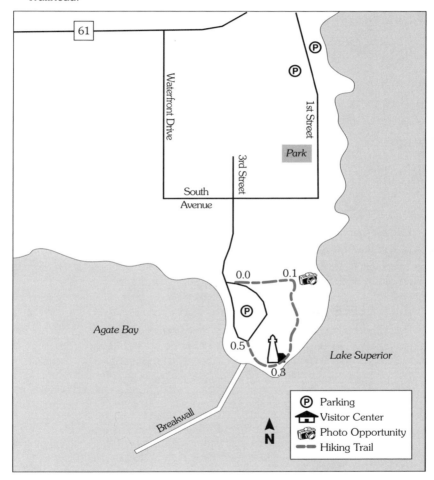

Foot Note:

Here's your chance to stay in a lighthouse—this one is also a Bed & Breakfast! Open year-round. Call 1-888-832-5606 for information.

SONJU HARBOR WALKING TRAIL

Burlington Bay to First Street
Two Harbors, MN • Off Highway 61, 26 miles from Duluth

- **Enjoyable views of Lake Superior can be seen from a shaded forest— right in town!**

- **On a hot summer day, this is a refreshing hike in the shade of towering pine, spruce, fir and birch at water's edge.**

- **Beautiful paved trail throughout—woods on one side, lake on the other.**

TRAILHEAD DIRECTIONS:
Highway 61 at mile marker 26.4 (Note: you will not find actual mile marker— use odometer reading from marker 25; after passing through the main area of town, watch for sign indicating Burlington Bay Campground), turn right onto First Street and follow for 0.1 mile to find ample parking in gravel lots on both sides of the street.

CONTACT:
Two Harbors Area Chamber of Commerce: 1-800-777-7384

TOTAL TRAIL LENGTH, SURFACE & WIDTH:
0.7 mile; paved; approximately 8' wide.

INCLINES & ALERTS:
No inclines greater than 10°. Some spur trails may have dropoffs; no guardrails.

TRAILHEAD FACILITIES & FEES:
No facilities at trailhead; however, flush toilets (seasonal) in picnic area across First Street at 0.1 mile. No fees for trail use.

MILEAGE & DESCRIPTION

0.0 Trailhead begins up hill from parking area (approximately 400') at sign indicating "No Unauthorized Vehicles in Park." A forest of spruce, pine and birch welcomes you. A turn in the trail gives way to the first of many benches placed in honor or memory of loved ones. Several spur trails throughout the remainder of this trail lead you to rest and soak up the sights, sounds and sweeping vistas of Lake Superior.

0.1 This section takes you past a small picnic area; a larger picnic area is located across First Street and is complete with playground equipment, a shelter and seasonal flush toilets. See Lakeview Park Picnic Area (pg. 164).

0.2 At Y in trail, notice a sign indicating restrooms (those described above). Further down the trail, additional benches and a scenic overlook await you.

0.3 When you reach the intersection with First Street (at the sidewalk), we suggest you turn around here and retrace path to trailhead. If you turn left and continue, you will eventually arrive at the parking area near the old lighthouse.

However, there is an easier way to get there—see pg. 52 for Sonju Harbor Walking Trail (Lighthouse Loop).

0.7   Trailhead

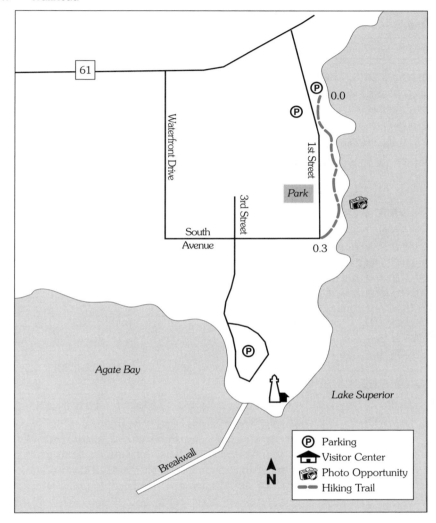

Gooseberry Falls State Park • On Highway 61, 39 miles from Duluth

- **See Gooseberry Falls from exceptional vantage points as a paved trail takes you to Upper and Lower Falls.**
- **Experience the magic of the North Shore's most visited waterfall!**

TRAILHEAD DIRECTIONS:

Highway 61 at mile marker 38.9, turn right into Gooseberry Falls State Park and follow signs to paved parking area.

CONTACT:

Gooseberry Falls State Park: (218) 834-3855

TOTAL TRAIL LENGTH, SURFACE & WIDTH:

0.7 mile; paved; average 6' wide (Note: All benches have pavement extended to them). The park states that this trail meets the standards for Universal Design.

INCLINES & ALERTS:

No inclines greater than 10°. Steep cliffs, no guardrails. Potential wet areas. Trail to Middle Falls only is cleared via snowblower in winter, but may have ice.

TRAILHEAD FACILITIES & FEES:

Simply some of the best the North Shore has to offer! Largest Visitor Center, gift shop, Interpretive Center. Flush toilets and water. Parking at Visitor Center is free for first two hours (for longer term parking, please use picnic area lot located 1 mile from Visitor Center). To park at picnic area or drive anywhere else in the park, an annual or day use state park permit is required and is available at the Visitor Center.

MILEAGE & DESCRIPTION

0.0 Trailhead begins at far end of Visitor Center on asphalt, then splits shortly. Continue straight following sign indicating Falls area.

0.1 At Y in trail, veer right following sign indicating "Middle & Lower Falls." In 70' find a bench to the left. Soon you will be making your way down to the impressive Middle Falls area. On this trail, there will be an option of steps or ramp to reach the Middle and Upper Falls. Mileage was calculated using the ramp.

There are 3 more benches along the switchback ramp and are placed approximately every 100'.

0.2 Excellent view of Middle Falls! The water levels fluctuate dramatically from raging torrents during spring runoff to ribbons during a dry summer season. From this area you can also hike to Lower Falls; however, the trail is not paved and there are steps with no ramp option.

On your journey to Upper Falls, you have two choices. The 60 steps (cement, double handrail, non-continuous) that you see on your return from Middle Falls will take you there or you can retrace path back to intersection and turn right following sign indicating Middle & Lower Falls.

0.4 Soon you will be walking beside Gooseberry River above the Middle Falls. Continue straight on asphalt path. Alert: Heed warning sign: "Please stay on trail – erosion is serious problem on steep hills. Keep young children in hand." The roaring cascades of the Upper Falls create an exceptional photo op.

In a few feet, pause to read the interpretive sign. Various North Shore rivers must carve their way through rock as they travel toward Lake Superior because of a phenomenon called uplift. Approximately 10,000 years ago, huge ice sheets put tremendous weight on the North Shore area and the land was actually sagging. When the ice receded, the earth literally sprang back up. Since Lake Superior was receding, the rivers were forced to cut through rock to reach it.

In a few more feet you will see a set of steps to the left. These lead to the Plaza Overlook Loop (pg. 58) and take you there by a more scenic route. To reach Upper Falls, continue straight on asphalt path.

0.5 Dramatic view of Upper Falls! Alert: Steep dropoff with no guardrail. This is a very popular photo op and many family pictures have been taken here.

The paved portion of the trail ends here, which concludes this hike. Turn around and follow paved path back to Visitor Center. Note: See Gooseberry River Loop (pg. 64) for continuation of this trail.

0.7 Visitor Center and trailhead.

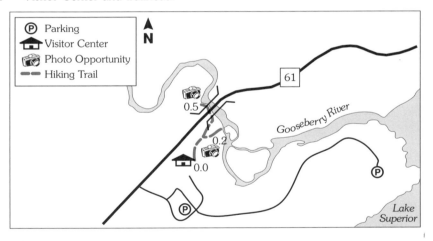

 Foot Note:

Gooseberry Falls State Park has the largest nature store on the North Shore. Proceeds from items purchased at all park gift shops help fund resource management and interpretive projects.

Current resource management projects underway at North Shore state parks include tree planting, river bank restoration and informational displays (kiosks).

Gooseberry Falls State Park • On Highway 61, 39 miles from Duluth

- **Information seekers' paradise! From historic facts about the park to the formation of Lake Superior's basin—it's all here and more.**
- **See 'Castle in the Park' and a remnant of the original bridge.**
- **One of the best vantage points for viewing Upper Falls with a beautiful vista of Gooseberry River—all from a paved trail.**

TRAILHEAD DIRECTIONS:
Highway 61 at mile marker 38.9, turn right into Gooseberry Falls State Park and follow signs to paved parking area.

CONTACT:
Gooseberry Falls State Park: (218) 834-3855

TOTAL TRAIL LENGTH, SURFACE & WIDTH:
0.6 mile; paved; average 6–8' wide (Note: All benches have pavement extended to them). The park states that this trail meets the standards for Universal Design.

INCLINES & ALERTS:
No inclines greater than 10°. Trail is not cleared in winter. Information boards are covered in winter.

TRAILHEAD FACILITIES & FEES:
Simply some of the best the North Shore has to offer! Largest Visitor Center, gift shop, Interpretive Center. Flush toilets and water. Parking at Visitor Center is free for first two hours (for longer term parking, please use picnic area lot located 1 mile from Visitor Center). To park at picnic area or drive anywhere else in the park, an annual or day use state park permit is required and is available at the Visitor Center.

MILEAGE & DESCRIPTION

0.0   Trailhead begins at far end of Visitor Center on blacktop path. In 80', trail splits; veer left following sign toward Plaza and Bridge Overlook. Pass through a stand of cedar and aspen.

0.1   Bench on left side. The huge wall to the left is the Plaza Wall that borders the Plaza Overlook. The Plaza Wall is more than 300' long.

In 100', find another bench on the right and a third one just before the steps. Ramp to Plaza is to the left; however, continue straight on blacktop for now. We will access the Plaza Overlook via a different route as famous views of Upper Falls and Gooseberry River await.

After crossing under Highway 61, turn right onto wide cement bridge (iron guardrails) located directly below Highway 61.

0.2   It is definitely worth spending some time here. This bridge offers an exceptional vantage point for viewing Upper Falls and Gooseberry River—beautiful views on either side of bridge.

At end of bridge, turn right and follow pavement as trail parallels Highway 61. Continue on pedestrian path over the bridge.

0.3 Spend a little time as you cross this bridge (double guardrail) and enjoy a charming sight: Gooseberry River creates an interesting scene as it negotiates rocks and boulders—worth the traffic noise for this view! Lake Superior provides a splendid backdrop.

The interpretive sign reveals that Lake Superior is home to two types of salmon–Chinook and Coho–and four types of trout–Brook, Brown, Lake and Rainbow.

At end of bridge, turn left onto the Plaza Overlook. The signs along the way give history and trivia about this area, including:

Gooseberry Falls State Park was created in the 1930s.

Today the North Shore hosts thousands of visitors and is growing in popularity each year. It all started in 1920.

Throughout the year, Gooseberry Falls fluctuates from low to high depending on the amounts of rainfall.

The original bridge was built in 1925. Check out the remnant on display.

0.4 As you leave Plaza Overlook, you can read more about the 'Castle in the Park'. Have more fun discovering North Shore trivia.

Some of the quarried rocks weigh more than 7 tons.

As you continue your descent, another interpretive sign awaits. This one gives information on how the wall was built.

0.5 At intersection, turn right and follow signs to Visitor Center.

0.6 Visitor Center and trailhead.

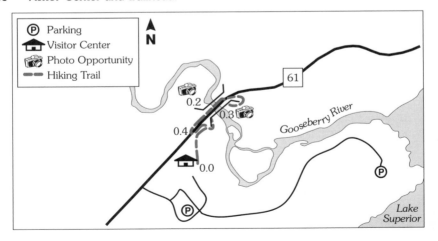

Gooseberry Falls State Park • On Highway 61, 39 miles from Duluth

- **Depending on the time of year and foliage bloom, constant views of Gooseberry River may be present.**
- **An impressive distant view of Gooseberry Falls.**
- **A great place to watch waves crash on Lake Superior's rugged shoreline.**

TRAILHEAD DIRECTIONS:
Highway 61 at mile marker 38.9, turn right into Gooseberry Falls State Park and follow signs to paved parking area.

CONTACT:
Gooseberry Falls State Park (218) 834-3855

TOTAL TRAIL LENGTH, SURFACE & WIDTH:
1.5 miles; hardpacked dirt and gravel; average 3–4' wide. Minimal rock and root.

INCLINES & ALERTS:
There are two inclines at 20° within 200' of each other and measure 20' and 15' respectively at 1.0 mile. Steep cliffs with no guardrail. Basalt lava flow-type rock may be slippery when wet.

TRAILHEAD FACILITIES & FEES:
Simply some of the best the North Shore has to offer! Largest Visitor Center, gift shop, Interpretive Center. Flush toilets and water. Parking at Visitor Center is free for first two hours (for longer term parking, please use picnic area lot located 1 mile from Visitor Center). To park at picnic area or drive anywhere else in the park, an annual or day use state park permit is required and is available at the Visitor Center.

MILEAGE & DESCRIPTION

0.0 Trailhead begins at Visitor Center. Follow sign indicating campground. By entering at this point, you will bypass many steps.

0.1 At trail intersection, continue straight. Watch for sign indicating campground. Listen for falls; nice views (foliage dependent) to left.

0.2 At next intersection, turn left and descend 20 steps (wood, no handrail, non-continuous); turn right at base. Great view of middle falls in the distance (view of lower falls is foliage dependent).

0.3 Ascend 7 uneven steps (stone, no handrail). Atop steps, continue straight. Do NOT take the next set of stone steps leading right. Short section of boardwalk further along on the trail.

0.6 In this section are two steep declines within 200' of each other. These are the inclines you will encounter at 1.0 mile on the return trail.

0.7 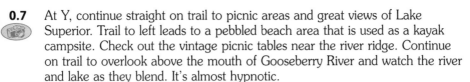 At Y, continue straight on trail to picnic areas and great views of Lake Superior. Trail to left leads to a pebbled beach area that is used as a kayak campsite. Check out the vintage picnic tables near the river ridge. Continue on trail to overlook above the mouth of Gooseberry River and watch the river and lake as they blend. It's almost hypnotic.

0.8 You have the option to continue on to the picnic shelter and more dramatic views of Superior's rugged shore by ascending the 20 steps (quarried rock, handrail) at the trail's end. Numerous photo ops abound in this area. Have fun exploring!

Vault toilet near parking entrance of picnic shelter. Flush toilets (seasonal) available at back of shelter. This shelter can also be reached by car. See Gooseberry Falls Picnic Areas (pg. 166).

After you've finished exploring this area, return to main trail and retrace path to trailhead.

1.0 This section contains the areas of steepest incline as mentioned in 0.6 above. The first is 20° for 20' with trail surface of hardpacked gravel. The second is 20° for 15' with trail surface of solid rock. Alert: Slippery when wet or icy.

1.5 Trailhead.

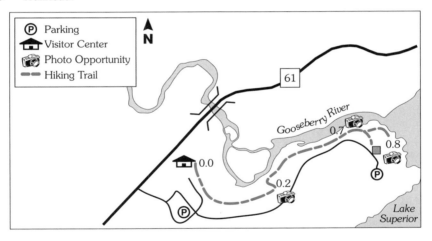

 **SAYS WHO?**

Want to reduce your risk of getting cancer?

Physical activity such as walking may reduce the risk for colon cancer as much as 50%.

Harvard Women's Health Watch [6,9]

Gooseberry Falls State Park • On Highway 61, 39 miles from Duluth

- **Spectacular vistas of Lake Superior crashing (or lapping) its rugged shoreline!**
- **Dynamic views of Gooseberry River as it flows into Lake Superior.**
- **Outstanding vantage point for viewing Upper Falls is en route to the official trailhead.**

TRAILHEAD DIRECTIONS:
Highway 61 at mile marker 38.9, turn right into Gooseberry Falls State Park and follow signs to paved parking area.

CONTACT:
Gooseberry Falls State Park: (218) 834-3855

TOTAL TRAIL LENGTH, SURFACE & WIDTH:
2.0 miles; paved first 0.2 mile; average 8' wide. Hardpacked dirt and gravel; average 1–2' wide. Minimal root and rock (moderate at times).

INCLINES & ALERTS:
There are five inclines ranging from 12–18°. Steepest is 18° for 45' at 1 mile. Longest is 16° for 75' at 1.2 miles. Steep cliffs and loose gravel (including vista overlooks) with no guardrails accompanied by eroding soil beneath. Vegetation overgrowth may be problematic in summer.

TRAILHEAD FACILITIES & FEES:
Simply some of the best the North Shore has to offer! Largest Visitor Center, gift shop, Interpretive Center. Flush toilets and water. Parking at Visitor Center is free for first two hours (for longer term parking, please use picnic area lot located 1 mile from Visitor Center). To park at picnic area or drive anywhere else in the park, an annual or day use state park permit is required and is available at the Visitor Center.

MILEAGE & DESCRIPTION

0.0   Official trailhead actually begins at 0.3 mile; however, the best route is to start at the far end of Visitor Center on blacktop path. This distance is included in total trail length.

In 80' trail splits; veer left following sign toward Plaza and Bridge Overlook. Pass through a stand of cedar and aspen.

0.1   Bench on left side. The huge wall to the left is the Plaza Wall, which borders the Plaza Overlook. In 100', find another bench on the right and a third one just before the stairs. Continue on blacktop (do not go up or down any stairs). Views of Gooseberry River and Upper Falls begin!

After passing under Highway 61, turn right onto wide cement bridge (iron rails) located directly below Highway 61.

0.2 Definitely worth spending some time here! This bridge offers an exceptional vantage point for viewing Upper Falls and Gooseberry River. Breathtaking views on either side of bridge.

At the end of bridge, follow sign to Gitchi Gummi trail by turning right. Continue on blacktop, taking the second trail on right marked by blue Hiking Club sign. Follow sign to Gitchi Gummi Trail as surface changes to hardpacked dirt and gravel. Enter forest of spruce, aspen and birch.

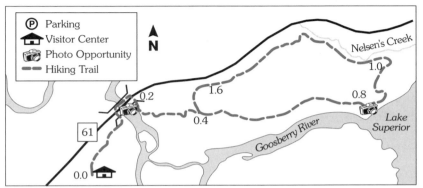

0.3 At Y in trail, veer left. Follow sign to Gitchi Gummi Trail. Traverse a few sections of boardwalk en route to a very nice stand of birch. Over the next 200', ascend two sets of steps—11 and 7 respectively (stone, wood, no handrail). Depending on foliage, vistas of Lake Superior come into view.

0.4 At next Y in trail, find sign stating "Hazardous. Keep children in hand." Trail map at this location. Continue straight (trail to the left eventually returns to this point). Traverse more boardwalk en route to incredible vista further up the path!

0.8 The introduction to this spectacular overlook is a rustic stone shelter (benches inside) that not only serves as a resting place, but provides great framing for photos! Alert: Although this is a beautiful vista, loose gravel and steep cliffs (no guardrail) mandate caution.

Depending on wind direction, you could be viewing Gooseberry River flowing into Lake Superior or vice-versa. Spend some time here absorbing the sights and sounds of the world's largest freshwater lake as it crashes (or laps) the rugged coastline. The park's designated picnic area is across the river.

0.9 In 200' find 18° decline with surface of hardpacked dirt and gravel.

1.0 This section contains the area of steepest incline on the trail (18° for 45') followed shortly by another 18° decline. Nelsen's Creek is just yards away. Views may tease or deliver, depending on foliage.

1.2 A gradual incline takes you closer to Highway 61.

1.6 Another trail shelter with benches inside signals a return (in 150') to the previously mentioned hazardous warning sign. At trail intersection, turn right and retrace path to trailhead.

2.0 Trailhead and Visitor Center.

Gooseberry Falls State Park • On Highway 61, 39 miles from Duluth • *Gentle Hikes name

- **Dramatic views of Upper Gooseberry Falls!**
- **Hike along the delightful Gooseberry River through a mixed forest, then onto a section of the Superior Hiking Trail.**

TRAILHEAD DIRECTIONS:
Highway 61 at mile marker 38.9, turn right into Gooseberry Falls State Park and follow signs to paved parking area.

CONTACT:
Gooseberry Falls State Park: (218) 834-3855

TOTAL TRAIL LENGTH, SURFACE & WIDTH:
1.2 miles; hardpacked dirt and gravel; average 3–4' wide. Minimum rock; moderate root. Second half of trail is primarily boardwalk.

INCLINES & ALERTS:
No inclines greater than 10°. Steep cliffs near upper falls (no guardrails). Potential wet areas.

TRAILHEAD FACILITIES & FEES:
Simply some of the best the North Shore has to offer! Largest Visitor Center, gift shop, Interpretive Center. Flush toilets and water. Parking at Visitor Center is free for first two hours (for longer term parking, please use picnic area lot located 1 mile from Visitor Center). To park at picnic area or drive anywhere else in the park, an annual or day use state park permit is required and is available at the Visitor Center.

MILEAGE & DESCRIPTION

0.0   Trailhead begins at far end of Visitor Center on asphalt, then splits shortly; continue straight following sign toward Falls area.

0.1   At second Y, follow sign to Upper Falls. Do not go up or down any steps; continue on asphalt. You will be walking beside Gooseberry River above Middle Falls.

0.2   Dramatic view of Upper Falls! (Alert: Steep dropoff with no guardrail).

Paved trail ends and rock/root surface begins (significant but flat bedrock is easily negotiable). Stay on trail near river. In 200', you will find a stone monument and warning sign. Trail surface changes to hardpacked gravel. At trail intersection, turn right.

Depending on river level, a Y in trail may be present shortly. If so, choose either as paths reconnect further on and continue parallel to river.

0.5   At next trail intersection, turn right and cross wide bridge (wood, double steel railing). Great photo ops up- and downriver. Immediately after crossing bridge, turn right onto boardwalk. This 0.3 mile section is part of the Superior Hiking Trail and will follow along above the Gooseberry River.

0.6 In this section you will encounter steps in the following series: Descend six (wood, no handrail, non-continuous); in 400' ascend 16 steps (wood, no handrail, non-continuous).

0.7 Look right for photo op upriver. In this section you will encounter the following series: Ascend four steps (wood, no handrail, non-continuous); five steps, cross small wooden bridge, then ascend nine steps (wood, no handrail).

0.8 Continue on boardwalk, then descend 13 steps (wood), cross bridge (wood, double handrail), then ascend four steps (wood).

0.9 At big pine surrounded by birch and spruce, look left to see SHT sign. Walk left toward sign, then turn right at trail intersection. In 200' find multi-path junction; follow signs to Visitor Center. Shortly, grassy trail meets asphalt near Fall View Shelter. Continue on asphalt. You can see Highway 61 to the left. In another short distance, a spur to right leads across a bridge (wood, double handrail) to natural rock overlook.

1.0 Back on asphalt, turn right at bridge that runs under Highway 61. Definitely worth spending some time here! This bridge offers an exceptional vantage point for viewing Upper Falls and Gooseberry River. Breathtaking views on either side of bridge. At trail intersection, turn left and cross under highway.

1.1 Pass stairs on the right and left, with bench at base of Plaza steps; continue straight. At Y in trail, follow sign to Visitor Center. In 200', find bench to your left. Another 100' further will be a bench to your right.

1.2 Visitor Center and trailhead.

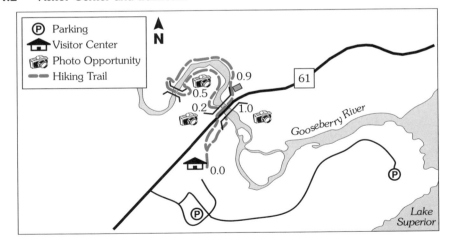

LITTLE TWO HARBORS PAVED TRAIL

Split Rock Lighthouse State Park • On Highway 61, 46 miles from Duluth

- **Stroll the paved section of the longer Little Two Harbors Trail through a lovely birch forest.**

- **Pack a picnic lunch and chose your favorite table with lake or wooded views, including a Piney Island vista.**

TRAILHEAD DIRECTIONS:

Highway 61 at mile marker 45.9, turn right into Split Rock Lighthouse State Park. Follow past Visitor Center turning right onto the first street you encounter. Follow for 0.5 mile to paved parking lot near sign indicating Pebble Beach Picnic Area.

CONTACT:

Split Rock Lighthouse State Park: (218) 226-6372.

TOTAL TRAIL LENGTH, SURFACE & WIDTH:

0.4 mile; paved; average 8' wide.

INCLINES & ALERTS:

No inclines greater than 10°. Pavement does not extend to picnic areas on this trail, but there are fully paved shelters (see Trail Center/Lakeview Picnic Area pg. 167). Spur trails are not paved.

TRAILHEAD FACILITIES & FEES:

Vault toilet at trailhead. Flush toilets and water in enclosed shelter. Annual or day use state park permit is required and is available at the park office.

MILEAGE & DESCRIPTION

0.0   Trailhead begins at southwest corner of parking area on asphalt path near vault toilet. Follow pavement for 100'. At intersection turn left and stay on paved trail. Right turn takes you to Pebble Beach (see pg. 136 for Pebble Beach Almost Hike). This trail has several optional, unpaved spurs (to the right) leading to the lakeshore. There are several picnic tables scattered about. If you brought picnic supplies, stop and enjoy this cool shaded area. Next you will cross a small bridge (wood, no handrails).

0.1   Enjoy hiking through a splendid stand of birch. Split Rock Lighthouse State Park has so much beauty to offer.

0.2   Pavement ends at the back of the building to the left. This building houses the Lakeview Picnic Shelter and Trail Center. Flush toilets and water are located inside. At this point, turn around and retrace path to trailhead or continue on Little Two Harbors Trail (pg. 68).

0.4   Trailhead

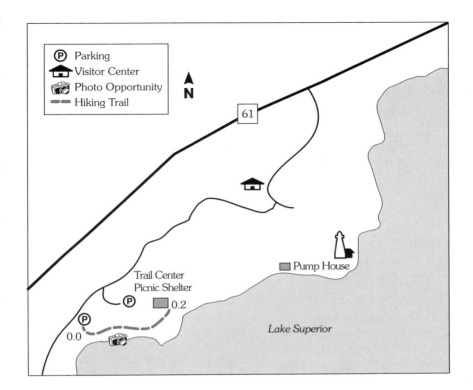

Birch trees can die when their bark is stripped.

![Owl icon] **SAYS WHO?**

Want to reduce your risk for osteoporosis?

Walk briskly. Women who exercise have a lower risk of developing osteoporosis.

Harvard Women's Health Watch [6]

LITTLE TWO HARBORS TRAIL

Split Rock Lighthouse State Park • On Highway 61, 46 miles from Duluth

- **Birch lovers' paradise! Hike through this stunning forest that leads to Split Rock Lighthouse.**
- **Several spur trails lead to dramatic lighthouse views and historic sites.**
- **Our cover photo was shot on this hike.**

TRAILHEAD DIRECTIONS:

Highway 61 at mile marker 45.9, turn right into Split Rock Lighthouse State Park. Follow past Visitor Center turning right onto the first street you encounter. Follow for 0.4 mile and turn left at sign indicating Trail Center and Lakeview Picnic Area.

CONTACT:

Split Rock Lighthouse State Park: (218) 226-6372

TOTAL TRAIL LENGTH, SURFACE & WIDTH:

0.8 mile; gravel and hardpacked dirt; average 6–8' wide.

INCLINES & ALERTS:

There is one incline of 14° for 25' at 0.2 mile. Optional spur trails may lead to rocky and uneven surfaces.

TRAILHEAD FACILITIES & FEES:

Flush toilets and water in enclosed shelter. Annual or day use state park permit is required and is available at the park office.

MILEAGE & DESCRIPTION

0.0 Trailhead begins off pavement at back of enclosed picnic shelter (south corner) near sign for Little Two Harbors Trail and Lighthouse. Various spur trails lead you to dramatic lighthouse views and historical sights on the rocky shore of Lake Superior.

Enter what we consider the most stunning stand of birch among our hikes! Complemented with spruce, this trail is gorgeous every season of the year. Next you will cross a bridge (wood, double handrails).

0.2 In this section you will encounter the area of steepest incline (14° for 25') as you continue to hike through this striking forest of birch, spruce and fir.

0.3 Bench to your left and an intersection. The spur to the right leads to the lake, pump house and dock site. Continuing on, find another bench and intersection. This spur will take you to the old tramway (used 1916–1934) and a picnic table.

0.4 Pavement begins. If you continue another 200', you will arrive at the History Center and gift shop (there is also a gift shop at the park office. Seasonal tours of the lighthouse are available. To complete this trail, turn around and retrace path to trailhead.

0.8 Trailhead

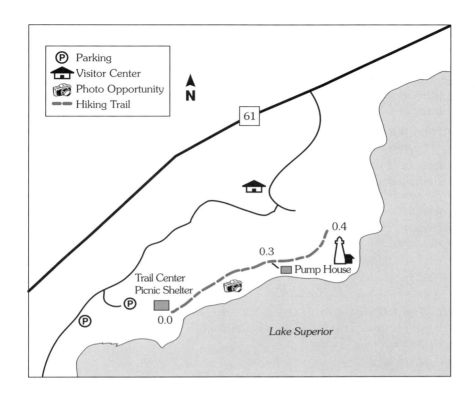

Foot Note:

MN Historical Society offers seasonal tours of Split Rock Lighthouse, which was built in 1910. Call for more information: (218) 226-6372 or www.mnhs.org.

SHT Section: Beaver Bay to Silver Bay
Off Highway 61, approximately 51 miles from Duluth

- **Hike along Beaver River, which begins calm and sedate but gradually turns into thundering falls!**

- **Enjoy the coolness of the forest glade as you pass through dense stands of fir and cedar.**

- **At falls of Beaver River, notice the abundance of kettles in the rock. Falls range from ribbons to rapids.**

TRAILHEAD DIRECTIONS:
Highway 61 at mile marker 51.1, turn left onto County Road 4 (Lax Lake Road) and follow for 0.6 miles. Look to the right for a small SHT sign along road. Turn right into gravel parking area.

CONTACT:
Superior Hiking Trail: (218) 834-2700

TOTAL TRAIL LENGTH, SURFACE & WIDTH:
2.0 miles; hardpacked dirt; starts out about 6–8' wide, but decreases to 1–2'. Moderate rock and root.

INCLINES & ALERTS:
There are six inclines ranging from 14–20°. The steepest and longest is 20° for 60' located at 0.8 miles. The following are applicable for the first 0.3 mile: Multi-use trail shared with ATVs, very muddy when wet, may have standing water in sections. River trail is easy to miss at end of bridge. Overgrowth may be problematic in summer. Some trail erosion along river. Unsecured laid-log section. After 0.8 mile, steep cliffs with no guardrail.

TRAILHEAD FACILITIES & FEES:
No facilities available. No fees for trail use.

MILEAGE & DESCRIPTION

0.0 Trailhead begins at far end of parking area near sign exhibiting SHT logo. No trail names are indicated. Off to the left notice two settling ponds as you walk along a wide rock and gravel roadbed. Alert: This part of the trail is shared with ATVs. Also, it can be very muddy if wet.

0.3 Cross wide bridge over Beaver River (steel, double guardrails). Do NOT continue to follow ATV trail. You will leave the trail and turn right onto a narrow trail approximately 4' wide immediately after crossing the bridge. This trail is easy to miss, especially in summer when overgrowth is prevalent.

You are now traveling directly alongside Beaver River. Use caution as trail erosion is present. Foliage-dependent views tease or please.

0.4 A wonderfully shaded section of fir serves as a welcome respite on a hot summer day. Keep watch for the pine growing from atop a fern-covered boulder further down the trail. Soon, moss-covered boulders welcome you to yet another stand of shady fir.

0.6 As you enter a majestic cedar grove, there is a campsite to the left. Nice views of the river here. Further on there is an unsecured laid-log path.

0.8 Area of steepest incline (20° for 60'). As you begin to ascend the ridge, river activity increases. Look for mature pines and cedars lining the gorge.

0.9 Good view of rapids from the forested ridge. Descend 4 steps (stone, no handrail). Shortly you will enter a section of moderate rock.

1.0 Beaver River campsite: A beautiful, open campsite surrounded by cedar, fir and birch with the comforting murmur of Beaver River. Just beyond this campsite, there is a trail to the right that leads to rocks overlooking small waterfalls. Alert: Steep dropoffs with no guardrails; rock and root. Use caution if you decide to explore this area.

Majestic rock face above the falls supports a bounty of cedar. Depending on water levels, the falls range from ribbons to rapids. If you enjoy rock kettles, this is a great place to view them as they are in abundance. Turn around and retrace path to trailhead.

2.0 Trailhead

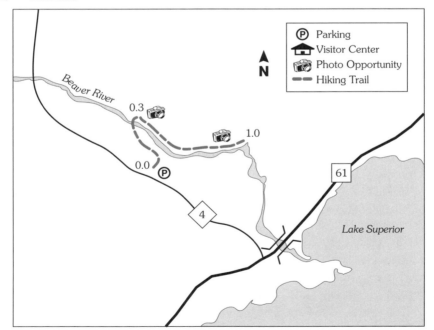

- **Each of these three easy trails leads through a forest to a different overlook: Silver Bay highlights, a sweeping vista of Lake Superior or an inland forest. See one or see them all!**

- **Find out about Northshore Mining, Lake Superior and her shipwrecks, as well as the city of Silver Bay.**

TRAILHEAD DIRECTIONS:

Highway 61 at mile marker 54.3 in Silver Bay (Note: There is a sign indicating "Scenic Overlook 1/2 mile" preceding marker); turn left onto Outer Drive (at traffic light). Follow for 0.6 mile, watching for sign on right indicating Scenic Overlook. Turn left toward solid waste recycling station (there is no street sign). Follow Scenic Overlook sign 0.3 mile to paved parking area. A lower lot provides RV parking.

CONTACT:

Silver Bay Information Center (seasonal): (218) 226-3143

TOTAL TRAIL LENGTH, SURFACE & WIDTH:

0.5 mile total for all three trails; gravel; average 5–6' wide.

INCLINES & ALERTS:

There are two inclines of 12°. Longest is 15' at 0.3 mile.

TRAILHEAD FACILITIES & FEES:

No facilities available. No fees for trail use

MILEAGE & DESCRIPTION

0.0 Trailhead begins in parking lot at sign indicating Plant View #1. It is about 90' to first overlook of Lake Superior and Northshore Mining plant with an informative interpretive display showing the various steps involved in taconite production. More than 4 million tons of taconite pellets are shipped across the Great Lakes yearly.

As you continue on trail toward parking lot, descend 4 steps (wood, no handrail).

0.1 Lake View #2 begins at far left corner of parking lot with sign indicating Views 2 & 3.

At trail intersection, find sign indicating Lake View; turn right. From the overlook you can see Palisade Head and beyond that to Shovel Point at Tettegouche State Park. There is interesting historical information about the shipwrecks of the *Hesper* and *Madeira*, both of which sank in 1905. Please note the information board for other points of interest, such as this tidbit: It takes a ship 7 days to get to the Atlantic Ocean from Lake Superior.

0.2   Back at intersection, take a right and follow the sign indicating City View #3.

0.3   This overlook provides you with a panorama of the city of Silver Bay. See the information board for various points of interest. Return to trail and at intersection turn right toward parking lot. This section of the trail has nice views of Lake Superior. The area of steepest incline (12° for 15') is in this section.

0.4   Parking lot and trailhead.

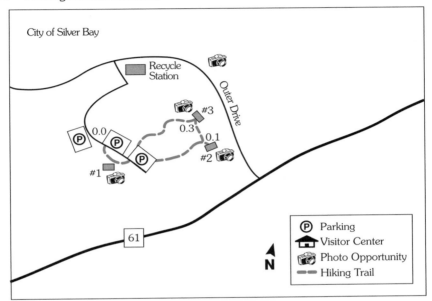

Foot Note:

To find out more information about all there is to do and see in Silver Bay, visit www.silverbay.com.

Tettegouche State Park • On Highway 61, 58 miles from Duluth • *Gentle Hikes name

- **Three overlooks with commanding views! See the towering Palisade Head—a 320' rhyolite cliff, sea caves and Shovel Point all along Lake Superior's rugged coastline.**

- **Wonderful picnic areas are scattered about, with access from this trail.**

TRAILHEAD DIRECTIONS:
Highway 61 at mile marker 58.5, turn right into Tettegouche State Park and follow road to paved parking area straight ahead. There is also a paved parking lot for RVs near the recycle bins.

CONTACT:
Tettegouche State Park: (218) 226-6365

TOTAL TRAIL LENGTH, SURFACE & WIDTH:
0.3 mile; paved; average 4' wide.

INCLINES & ALERTS:
There is one incline of 12° (21% grade) for 10' in the first section. Although paved, surface is rough and uneven in places.

TRAILHEAD FACILITIES & FEES:
Visitor Center with gift shop, informational displays, flush toilets and water fountain. This area also features a picnic area (see Tettegouche General Picnic Area pg. 168). Annual or day use state park permit is required and is available at the park office.

MILEAGE & DESCRIPTION

0.0 Trailhead begins at recycle bins on cement walk. As you follow the sidewalk, there will be several picnic tables facing parking area. At intersection, turn right onto asphalt path. Enter stand of maple. Picnic table to left on cement pad (pavement extends to table). Steepest area of incline (12° for 10'); roots through asphalt make surface uneven.

0.1 At intersection, continue on asphalt path, but first stop at overlook #1 (guardrail, benches) for commanding views of Palisade Head and sea caves. Continue on asphalt trail and in about 100' find another picnic table (pavement extends to table). At next intersection, stop at platform overlook #2 (guardrail) for a view of Lake Superior framed by birch and spruce. Continue straight on trail.

0.2 Unpaved spur trail leads to a wooded picnic area on your right. At the next intersection, continue straight to the platform overlook #3 (guardrail) and a dramatic view of Shovel Point and the nearby rocky outcrop. Go back to the intersection and turn left toward the Visitor Center. Grassy spur trails lead to additional picnic tables.

0.3 At intersection with road, turn right and head back toward the parking area.

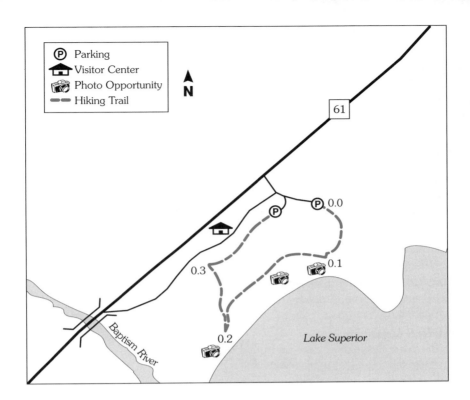

Feeling stressed-out? Get out and about!

Walking 30 minutes 4-6 days per week at a moderate pace can prevent or reduce stress and anxiety.

Exercising Your Way to Better Mental Health [19,20,21,22]

🌊 SHOVEL POINT TRAIL

Tettegouche State Park • On Highway 61, 58 miles from Duluth

- **This hike is on a peninsula and provides breathtaking views of Palisade Head, sea caves and rugged cliff faces!**
- **Aqua-blue waves crashing (or lapping) pink-tinted rhyolite cliffs combine for a remarkable scene.**
- **This is a popular spot for rock climbers.**

TRAILHEAD DIRECTIONS:
Highway 61 at mile marker 58.5, turn right into Tettegouche State Park and follow road to paved parking area straight ahead. There is also a paved parking lot for RVs near the recycle bins.

CONTACT:
Tettegouche State Park: (218) 226-6365

TOTAL TRAIL LENGTH, SURFACE & WIDTH:
1.4 miles; cement, asphalt, gravel and hardpacked dirt; average 2–4' wide. Minimal root and rock.

INCLINES & ALERTS:
There are five inclines ranging from 12–20°. Steepest is 20° for 20' at 0.8 mile. Steep cliffs—no guardrails. Keep children in hand.

TRAILHEAD FACILITIES & FEES:
Visitor Center with gift shop, informational displays, flush toilets and water fountain. Note: This area also features picnic areas (see Tettegouche General Picnic Areas pg. 168). Annual or day use state park permit is required and is available at the park office.

MILEAGE & DESCRIPTION

0.0 Official trailhead begins in 600'. For easy access, begin across the road from Visitor Center on wide cement walkway. As you head toward the lake, pass a picnic table to your left before coming to the first intersection, where the path changes to asphalt. Before turning left at this intersection, take a moment at this overlook (benches, guardrail).

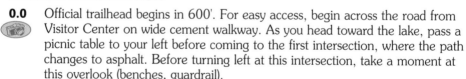

0.1 In this section, pass additional picnic sites surrounded by a mixed forest, some with lake views. The next intersection provides benches at a platform overlook (guardrail) offering commanding views of Palisade Head (an impressive cliff face with tall communications tower on top) and sea caves. Official trailhead for Shovel Point begins to the left of the information board; surface changes to gravel and hardpacked dirt.

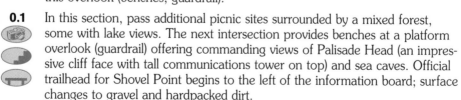

Descend 55 steps (wood, no handrail, non-continuous). This brings you to an intersection. To the left is Shovel Point trail. The path to the right (and down about 85 wooden steps) leads to a pebbled beach. Follow path to the left toward Shovel Point.

0.2 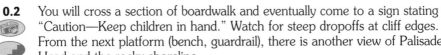 You will cross a section of boardwalk and eventually come to a sign stating "Caution—Keep children in hand." Watch for steep dropoffs at cliff edges. From the next platform (bench, guardrail), there is another view of Palisade Head and the rocky shoreline.

Throughout this section you will encounter steps (wood, handrail) in the following pattern: descend 3, then 14 (followed by wooden bridge, double handrail); ascend 19. At the intersection, take the spur to the right—descend 7 platform-type steps (wood, no handrail)—to a spectacular overlook (bench, guardrail) of a sea cave and stone arch.

Ascend 36 platform-type steps (wood, no handrail, non-continuous) that lead you through the woods. Ascend another 13 steps (wood, no handrail), then 46 steps (wood, no handrail, non-continuous).

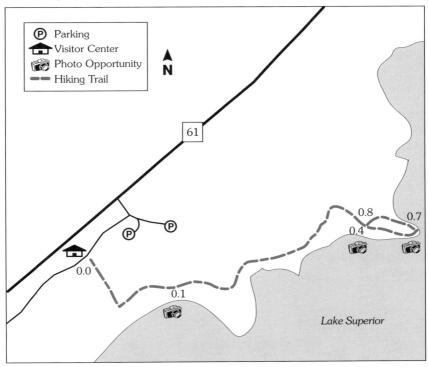

0.4 This section takes you up a rooted incline before ascending 32 steps (wood, handrail). Next, ascend a rocky, rooted incline that leads to another overlook (guardrail) and benches. The sights from these cliffs are some of the most frequently photographed and can be found on many postcards. To the left of the overlook is an area of cliffs often used by rock climbers.

0.5 Take the boardwalk from the overlook, cross the rock surface and then down several sets of steps (wood, no handrail, non-continuous). Notice the pines and cedars growing on the surface of the rock. Also note their shallow root system. High winds have felled many of these trees over the years.

Two additional overlooks (no guardrail) lead you to the cliff edge and many photo ops. After the steepest decline (16° for 35'), a spur trail to the right takes you to the cliff edge (no guardrail). Descend a set of 16 steps (wood, no handrail) to get there. Back on the trail, you will find two sections of boardwalk. Descend 5 steps (wood, no handrail).

0.7 A set of 26 steps (wood, double handrail) will bring you to a platform overlook (bench, guardrail) with stunning views of the bays and rocky coastline, which are so typical of the north shore of Lake Superior. Note the rugged, reddish rhyolite cliffs surrounding this point. Typically, the water is a beautiful shade of aqua-blue.

Back at the top of the steps, go straight, continuing across the rocky surface around the tip of the shovel. You will re-enter the wooded area atop the rock and hike through pine and cedar.

0.8 This section takes you up two areas of incline, which includes the area of steepest incline (20° for 20'), then brings you back to the main trail near the cliffs. Retrace path to trailhead.

1.4 Trailhead

SAYS WHO?

Feeling Blue? Get into the green.

Walking 30 minutes 4–6 days per week at a moderate pace can prevent or reduce depression.

Exercising Your Way to Better Mental Health [19,20,21,22]

High Falls at Tettegouche (see pg. 84) Photo by Melanie Morgan

Tettegouche State Park • On Highway 61, 58 miles from Duluth • *Gentle Hikes name

- **This beautiful wooded trail showcases the Baptism River as it is flows into Lake Superior.**
- **Dramatic view of Shovel Point and Lake Superior's rugged shoreline.**

TRAILHEAD DIRECTIONS:

Highway 61 at mile marker 58.5, turn right into Tettegouche State Park and follow road to paved parking area straight ahead. There is also a parking lot for RVs near the recycle bins.

CONTACT:

Tettegouche State Park: (218) 226-6365

TOTAL TRAIL LENGTH, SURFACE & WIDTH:

0.4 mile; cement, asphalt, gravel and hardpacked dirt; average 3–4' wide. Minimal rock and root.

INCLINES & ALERTS:

No inclines greater than 10°. No guardrails on some overlooks and trail sections.

TRAILHEAD FACILITIES & FEES:

Visitor Center with gift shop, informational displays, flush toilets and water fountain. Note: This area also features picnic areas (see Tettegouche General Picnic Areas pg. 168). Annual or day use state park permit is required and is available at the park office.

MILEAGE & DESCRIPTION

0.0   Trailhead begins across from Visitor Center on cement path. Picnic table with grill to left. At trail intersection, turn right onto asphalt path, but first stop at the overlook (guardrails) for views of Lake Superior framed by birch and spruce. Back on path, spur trail leads to wooded picnic areas on right.

0.1   At next intersection, continue straight. Stop at the platform overlook (guardrails) for a dramatic view of Shovel Point and the near rocky outcrops. Return to trail, which has now changed to gravel and hardpacked dirt. Descend 64 platform-type steps (wood, handrail, non-continuous).

0.2   This brings you to an intersection. If you descend the 11 steps (wood, handrail) to the left, you will have views of the mouth of the Baptism River (overlook, no guardrail) and Shovel Point. Back on the trail, descend 21 steps (wood, handrail). To the left and up, another 4 steps (wood, handrail) bring you to a bench and another view of the mouth of the Baptism River.

Next, descend 7 steps (wood, no handrail) to a platform path. A spur with 15 steps down (wood, no handrail) brings you to the sandbar at the beach.

Once again, return to the trail; notice the kayakers' information board regarding water trails. Turn left.

Continuing on the trail, you will encounter two optional spur trails—one takes you to the water's edge down 49 steps (wood, double handrail); the other takes you to a bench and overlook (guardrails), both with views up- and downriver. Continuing on the trail, you will cross a wooden bridge (double handrails) and ascend 49 steps (wood, handrail, non-continuous).

0.3 This brings you to the road and lower level parking area. Turn right and follow the walking path along the right side of the road.

0.4 Trailhead

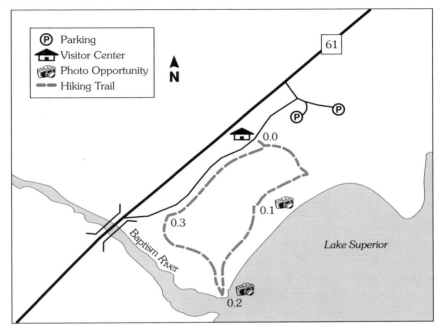

 **SAYS WHO?**

In a Bad Mood? Stride toward a better attitude!

Walking 30 minutes 4-6 days per week at a moderate pace can improve personality, mood, self esteem and well-being.

Exercising Your Way to Better Mental Health [19,20,21,22]

FISHERMAN'S TRAIL

Tettegouche State Park • On Highway 61, 58 miles from Duluth

- **Magnificent views of the Cascades await the eager adventurer!**
- **Views of the Baptism River are especially scenic after leaves have fallen.**

TRAILHEAD DIRECTIONS:
Highway 61 at mile marker 58.5, turn right into Tettegouche State Park and immediately take another right passing Visitor Center and follow for 0.1 mile to paved parking area (located on right side before crossing bridge).

CONTACT:
Tettegouche State Park: (218) 226-6365

TOTAL TRAIL LENGTH, SURFACE & WIDTH:
1.8 miles; hardpacked dirt and gravel; average 2' wide. Minimal rock and root.

INCLINES & ALERTS:
No inclines greater than 10°. Steep dropoffs with no guardrail at various sections of the trail. To get the best view of the Cascades, some moderate rock negotiation may be necessary.

TRAILHEAD FACILITIES & FEES:
Closest facilities are located at Visitor Center with gift shop, informational displays, flush toilets and water fountain. Annual or day use state park permit is required and is available at the park office.

MILEAGE & DESCRIPTION

0.0 Begin trailhead at left side of bridge on pedestrian path. While crossing the bridge, look left for a wonderful photo op of the Baptism River as it swirls through a rocky canyon en route to Superior. After crossing over bridge, turn right onto 6' wide hardpacked dirt trail and continue under Highway 61.

0.1 Look for a set of six wooden steps to your left. At this point, cross the road and find trailhead (there is no sign indicating Fisherman's Trail, but look for a greenish post with Brook Trout Regulation information. Trailhead is near guardrail ending). Over the next 200' you will descend 10 steps (wood, no handrail), then 12 steps (wood, handrail).

0.2 At trail intersection, turn left. This takes you along the Baptism River through a mixed forest. A couple of natural overlooks (no guardrail) afford wonderful views of the river. Further on, descend 9 steps (wood, no handrail) and cross a small bridge (wood, no handrail). Look for huge, moss-covered boulders throughout this area.

0.3 Bench to the right. If you desire to travel down to the river's edge, a spur trail to the right delivers in 26 steps (wood, no handrail). Nice views for photo ops.

Ascend 19 steps (wood, handrail, non-continuous). Further on, another spur trail to the right descends 19 steps (wood, no handrail) to a portion of rapids. Photos ops up- and downriver.

0.4 Descend seven steps (wood, no handrail). Check out the big boulders in the river! In 200', ascend 9 steps (wood, no handrail).

0.5 This section showcases some nice views overlooking the river. Over the next 250', descend 9 steps (wood, handrail). Further on, descend 5 steps (wood, no handrail). We saw Horsetail Plant in abundance at this spot on the trail. Cross small bridge (wood, no handrail).

0.6 Over the next 400', ascend 13 steps (wood, no handrail), cross bridge (wood, double handrail), then find boardwalk path.

0.7 This section contains numerous steps (all wood with no handrails) as follows: Ascend 23 (non-continuous); in a few yards, cross a bridge; descend 14, then descend another 6. Immediately cross another bridge, then ascend 45. In approximately 80', descend 22 (wood, handrail, non-continuous).

0.8 This section begins with a bridge leading to more steps (all wood with handrails). Cross bridge and immediately descend 12 steps. In 200', cross another bridge, then descend 19 steps (no handrail). Here the trail widens considerably to include the rocky river bed. Depending on water levels, partial views of the cascades at the trail's end may be seen by exploring this area.

0.9 The best view is a bit further. If you don't mind negotiating some small rocks (we picked the ones between the cedar and the birch), a spur trail will take you to a spectacular view of the Cascades! Magnificent photo ops await from that vantage point.

When you're ready, retrace path to trailhead.

1.8 Trailhead.

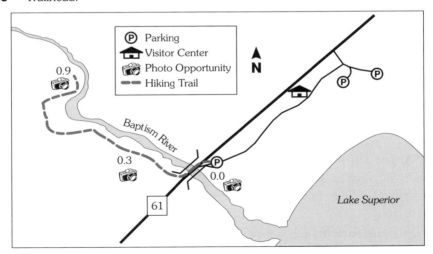

HIGH FALLS AT TETTEGOUCHE

Tettegouche State Park • On Highway 61, 58 miles from Duluth

- **Breathtaking views of the 80' High Falls.**
- **Phenomenal views of the Baptism River.**

TRAILHEAD DIRECTIONS:
Highway 61 at mile marker 58.5, turn right into Tettegouche State Park and immediately take another right passing Visitor Center. Trailhead is located 1.5 miles beyond Visitor Center. Drive downhill, cross bridge and follow signs to Trail Center where paved parking lot is located.

CONTACT:
Tettegouche State Park: (218) 226-6365

TOTAL TRAIL LENGTH, SURFACE & WIDTH:
1.6 miles; hardpacked dirt and gravel; 3–4' wide. Minimal rock and root.

INCLINES & ALERTS:
There are four inclines ranging from 12–16°. Steepest and longest: 16° for 45' at 1.2 miles. Very steep dropoff at viewing area for High Falls (no guardrail). Suspension bridge crossing permits no more than five persons at a time.

TRAILHEAD FACILITIES & FEES:
Vault toilet and picnic area (see High Falls Picnic Area pg. 169) nearby. Annual or day use state park permit is required and is available at the park office.

MILEAGE & DESCRIPTION

0.0 Trailhead begins from parking area at sign indicating "High Falls Trail." A portion of this trail is a SHT spur.

A forest of cedars scattered with alder greet you as you gradually ascend a 10° grade on a wide, fairly level path for the first 0.1 mile. Trail intersection in 250'. Continue straight.

0.1 Trail takes on more rock, but still good walking surface. Pines have joined the forest here.

0.2 At trail intersection, turn right and follow signs to High Falls (0.5 mile ahead). This is where the trail joins the SHT spur.

0.4 This section contains the steepest decline (16° for 45'). Soon a couple sections of boardwalk follow.

0.6 Shortly you will encounter a wooden platform and trail intersection with steps in both directions. Turn left here and descend 67 steps (wood, no handrail, non-continuous) that lead to an overlook of High Falls (foliage-dependent view).

Further along, descend 18 steps (wood, no handrail, non-continuous) and find a spur to the right equipped with boardwalk leading to an overlook (guardrail).

This overlook provides a dramatic view of the falls from a vantage point directly over them.

0.7 Back on the trail, descend 38 steps (wood, no handrail). Take care when descending the final step as it leads to uneven rock. Pick up trail to the left. Cross small bridge (wood, double handrail). Ascend 6 steps (wood, double handrail).

Make sure to look upriver for a gorgeous view of the Baptism River as you cross the suspension bridge. Once across the suspension bridge, you will encounter the following series of steps (wood, no handrail unless otherwise noted): ascend 12 (double handrail); descend 12; ascend 7.

Here is the best view of High Falls thus far on the trail. (Alert: Very steep cliff, no guardrails or platform). Officially we ended our portion of the trail here. Turn around at this point and retrace path to trailhead. However, there is an option* for a better view.

*Option: If you're up for the challenge of 184 steps (non-continuous), this option delivers a great view. You will encounter the following series of steps (all wood, no handrail, non-continuous): Ascend 28, descend 71, find bench (timely positioned), then descend the remaining 85 to the base of falls. At the base, you'll find the best view. But remember, what goes down must come up. If you do travel to the bottom of the falls, be certain to have your camera in hand. Spend some time scoping out the best shot. It's worth it!

1.2 Area of steepest incline 16° for 45'.

1.6 Trailhead

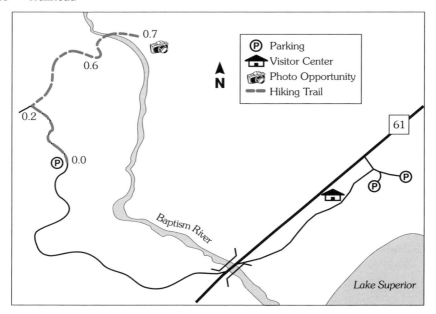

TETTEGOUCHE LAKE OVERLOOK

Tettegouche State Park • Off Highway 61, approximately 59 miles from Duluth

- **The view at the overlook is definitely worth the hike: Tettegouche Lake nestled among tamarack and mixed evergreens.**

- **This is one of the few trails featuring significant oak growth.**

- **Outdoor informational signs display facts about the trail, geology and forest of Tettegouche.**

TRAILHEAD DIRECTIONS:

Highway 61 at mile marker 59.3, turn left onto County Road 1 and follow for 4.3 miles. As you travel on County Road 1, mile markers will change. Prior to mile marker 343, watch for sign indicating Lake County Road 4 (Lax Lake Road). Turn left on County Road 4 and follow for 3 miles to gravel parking area on left (this lot is unmarked, but visible from the road; look for fire marker 5932).

CONTACT:

Tettegouche State Park: (218) 226-6365

TOTAL TRAIL LENGTH, SURFACE & WIDTH:

1.7 miles; gravel and hardpacked dirt; average 8' wide; spur to overlook 1–2' wide. Minimum root and rock.

INCLINES & ALERTS:

There is one incline of 12° for 85' at 0.2 mile. Entrance trail is service road shared by park personnel vehicles. Long, gradual incline of about 10° for the first 0.6 mile. Overlook has no guardrail. Although this trail meets the criteria for an easier rating, due to the length of its incline, we gave it a moderate rating.

TRAILHEAD FACILITIES & FEES:

No facilities available. Annual or day use state park permit is required and is available at the park office.

MILEAGE & DESCRIPTION

0.0   Trailhead begins from parking area at right of information board. This is a service road used by park personnel—watch for vehicles. There is a long, gradual incline of 10° for the first 0.6 mile of this trail.

0.2   Area of steepest incline (12° for 85').

0.3   Bench to left; informational marker telling about the rock found here. Rocks in this area are found in abundance on the moon but are very rare on Earth.

0.6   Bench to left; informational marker telling about the oaks in this park. Bears have traveled 20 miles to feast on the acorns from these oaks.

Look for trail sign. Spur trail to Tettegouche Lake Overlook is across the road from this bench. Spur trail is 1–2' wide and is gentle and flat. Late summer overgrowth may be possible. Oaks become even more prevalent in this area.

0.8 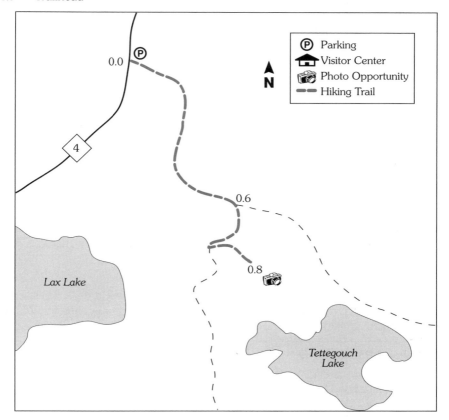 Cross one section of boardwalk. At trail intersection, find sign indicating Tettegouche Lake Overlook. Take spur trail to the left. This leads to an area overlooking Tettegouche Lake with Lake Superior in the distance (steep cliff, no guardrail). A natural rock formation sits about bench height for your viewing pleasure. Turn around and retrace path to trailhead. The roadway decline makes for a quick return.

1.7 Trailhead

George H. Crosby-Manitou State Park • Off Highway 61, approximately 59 miles from Duluth

- **Hike beneath a rocky ridge in the shade of maple, birch, fir and cedar along the shores of beautiful Bensen Lake.**

- **Remoteness, tranquility, a vibrant moss-covered forest floor: all these describe this pristine environment.**

TRAILHEAD DIRECTIONS:
Highway 61 at mile marker 59.3, turn left onto County Road 1 and follow for 6.2 miles (you will travel through Finland). Turn right onto County Road 7 and follow for 7.6 miles. Turn right onto Bensen Lake Road (also Fire #7616) into George H. Crosby-Manitou State Park and follow for 0.5 mile to gravel parking lot on left.

CONTACT:
This park is managed by Tettegouche State Park: (218) 226-6365

TOTAL TRAIL LENGTH, SURFACE & WIDTH:
1.1 miles; gravel roadway; average 10' wide, for 0.1 mile. Significant root and moderate rock for 0.5 mile through forest; average 1–3' wide. Boardwalk for second half of trail.

INCLINES & ALERTS:
No inclines greater than 10°. Watch for vehicles while walking on roadway. Small bridge along trail may be loose. Wet areas possible on trail.

TRAILHEAD FACILITIES & FEES:
Vault toilets at parking lot by informational signs and at picnic area (see Bensen Lake Picnic Area on pg. 170). Water (seasonal) available at park entrance. Annual or day use state park permit is required. A pay box is available at the entrance.

MILEAGE & DESCRIPTION

0.0   Trailhead begins at far end of parking area at sign on roadway indicating Bensen Lake Trail. Road is shared with vehicles going to picnic area at lakeshore.

0.1   Enter trail to left side of road preceding picnic area at sign indicating Bensen Lake Trail. Soon descend 3 steps (wood, no handrail), then cross small bridge (wood, no handrail).

Upon entering the first stand of fir, a sense of remoteness permeates the air. Pause for a moment, as this part of the forest is nearly suffused in green. Root and rock abound making for an uneven trail, but we found it worth the extra effort! Soon you'll be treading alongside the pristine beauty of Bensen Lake.

This side of the lake hosts several pack-in campsites located atop the ridge to your left. Continue straight on the trail.

0.2   This section has significant rock and root. Past campsite #22 you will find a small SHT sign posted on a tree. Continue walking along the lakeshore.

0.3 At the time of writing, a bubbling brook flowed from Bensen Lake and under the boardwalk. Shortly, you will ascend 4 steps (wood, no handrail). In less than 200', the Beaver Bog Trail will intersect your path. Park map is located to your right. Continue walking along the lakeshore. Alert: Small bridge may be loose.

0.6 The SHT and Matt Willis Trails intersect from the left; continue straight. Park map is located to your right. A few sections of boardwalk (may be loose) will bring you to an old beaver dam. Note that the forest has opened to a more shrubby area. You will pass campsite #19.

0.7 A long section of boardwalk (about 1,250') brings you back into the forest. This newer boardwalk protects the forest floor and carries you over probable wet areas as well.

0.9 The boardwalk will eventually transport you to the wooded picnic area that you bypassed when starting this hike. Continue walking to road and retrace path to trailhead.

1.1 Trailhead.

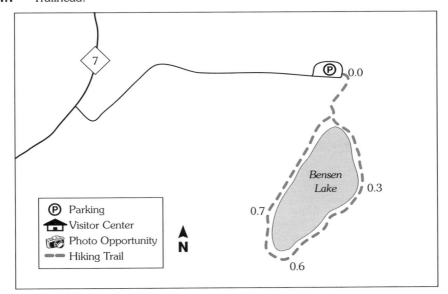

On Highway 61, 73 miles from Duluth

- **Allow plenty of time for this self-guided interpretive trail with many interesting features (guide booklets available in mailbox near parking area).**
- **This is the former site of a pulpwood rafting operation (1943–1971).**
- **Scientific and Natural Area with Native Plant Restoration Project underway.**

TRAILHEAD DIRECTIONS:

Highway 61 at mile marker 73.1, locate sign indicating 'Sugar Loaf Cove State Natural Area.' Look to the right and take the gravel entrance into Sugarloaf Cove (near fire number 9096).

CONTACT:

Sugarloaf Cove: (218) 879-4334

TOTAL TRAIL LENGTH, SURFACE & WIDTH:

1.0 mile; grass, gravel and hardpacked dirt; average 5' wide.

INCLINES & ALERTS:

There are two inclines ranging from 12–18°. Steepest incline is 18° for 35' at 0.9 mile. Some sections of trail have uneven surface. May be slippery in wet areas, especially on rocks. Please do not hike onto Sugarloaf Point as the vegetation is very fragile.

TRAILHEAD FACILITIES & FEES:

Interpretive Center (open on weekends, seasonal). No fees for trail use.

MILEAGE & DESCRIPTION

0.0 Trailhead starts at east end of parking area (may be marked by hay bales) at alder thicket. Although scenic and beautiful in its own right, this trail is best known for its interpretive features. Please make sure that you have picked up a trail guide from the mailbox by the Sugarloaf Cove sign in parking area. Numbers are the only thing posted on interpretive signs throughout the trail, so a guide booklet explaining them is a necessity.

#1 Relax on a bench and enjoy the cool freshness of a very dense stand of tall pine.

0.1 #2 Boom logs from pulpwood rafting operation

#3 Alder thicket. You will cross a bridge (no handrails), then enter an area of pine, alder and birch.

#4 Weathering bedrock

0.2 This section contains an area of decline.

#5 Watch and listen for birds as you enjoy this overlook among maples, spruce, birch, pine and alder. At trail intersection, turn right or take a left for option.

*Option: We made station #6 optional because the route to it exceeds our book criteria (decline/incline of 24° for 10'). You will also encounter an additional decline of 18° for 50', then travel over a somewhat rocky area if you take this option.

#6 Rocky cliffs

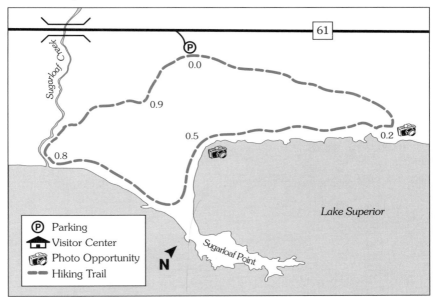

0.3 #7 Log chute. Find a bench nestled among spruce, pine and birch. Another area of decline.

0.4 #8 Nurse log. Minimum to moderate root in this area—watch your step.

#9 Rocky shoreline. As you walk through the woods, look for lichen (called Old Man's Beard) hanging from spruce trees. Another decline.

0.5 #10 Superintendent's house/office. All that remains today is the root cellar and portions of the house foundation. At intersection, notice the hand pump to the right—it still operates. Turn left toward the beach.

#11 Cobble beach. Take time to explore this beach, but please do not hike onto Sugarloaf Point due to its sensitive vegetation. Follow the shoreline to the area of bedrock at water's edge. Trail picks up to the right and re-enters the woods.

0.6 #12 Log rafts.

0.7 #13 Tombolo (wetland) area. A boardwalk has been placed to make your hike easier and more pleasant through this section.

#14 Mouth of stream. Trail follows along stream, then brings you to an area of incline (12° for 10').

#15 Old beach line and boom logs.

0.9 Area of steepest incline (18° for 35').

 #16 Beach terrace. Two benches give you opportunity to pause as you look toward Sugarloaf Point and the pine plantings. When you resume your hike, you enter the dark beauty of the pine plantation created by the paper company when they closed their rafting operation in 1971.

#17 Interpretive center. The center is typically open on weekends (seasonal) and provides a great place to learn more about this unique area. Bring a lunch to enjoy at your leisure (picnic tables provided) and observe the various elements that live in this ecosystem.

1.0 Return to parking area.

SAYS WHO?

Got a craving that just won't relent, even though your caloric intake has already been spent?

Studies demonstrate that exercise can reduce cravings for high fat or high sugar snack foods.

Psychology Today [14]

Temperance River (see pg. 96). Photo by Melanie Morgan

SHT Section: Cook County Road 1 to Temperance River State Park
Off Highway 61, approximately 79 miles from Duluth

- **Colorful fungal growth abounds throughout this scientific area with its intriguing variety of flora.**
- **Quaint creeks and moss-covered logs showcase nature's splendor.**
- **The Superior Hiking Trail Association considers this to be a great fall color hike culminating in a natural overlook of Lake Superior and Finland State Forest below.**

TRAILHEAD DIRECTIONS:
Highway 61 at mile marker 78.9 (across from Lamb's Resort and before Cross River Wayside), turn left on County Road 1 and follow for 3.7 miles. Look for fire marker indicating 'Cramer Road #843' on the right and park in gravel area for SHT.

CONTACT:
Superior Hiking Trail: (218) 834-2700

TOTAL TRAIL LENGTH, SURFACE & WIDTH:
2.8 miles; hardpacked dirt; average 1–2' wide. Moderate root and rock in first 0.2 mile.

INCLINES & ALERTS:
There are 12 inclines ranging from 14–20°. Steepest and longest incline is 20° for 90' at 1.1 miles. No guardrails at overlook. Wet and muddy areas possible. Boardwalk and cut-log paths may be loose. All are very slippery when wet and may be challenging to navigate. Vegetation overgrowth possible in late summer season.

TRAILHEAD FACILITIES & FEES:
No facilities available. No fees for trail use.

MILEAGE & DESCRIPTION

0.0 Trailhead begins off parking area at SHT sign (no notation for Tower Overlook; follow sign toward Cross River). Enter through a stand of birch, which changes to a mixed forest. Listen for sounds of a river as you hike this section. Vegetation overgrowth may be possible in late season. Notice Old Man's Beard lichen hanging in trees.

0.3 In this area, you will encounter more than 150' of boardwalk. Take note of interesting mushrooms and other fungal growth along the trail.

0.6 You will cross a cut-log footpath in this section.

0.7 Boardwalk paths cross a couple small creeks.

0.9 In this area you will cross a few sections of cut-log path, encounter moderate rock and root and more boardwalk paths. You will find an area of rhyolite (the reddish, angular rock) as the trail meanders through the forest.

1.0 Shortly, you will cross a footbridge (no handrail) that provides a lovely summer photo op upstream.

1.1 Cross additional sections of cut-log path. This section contains the area of steepest incline (20° for 90').

1.4 A gradual descent to an open rock surface brings you to a wide, open expanse overlooking the Finland State Forest below. Looking toward Lake Superior, you can see the towers of Taconite Harbor and a breathtaking view of the lake. To the right is George H. Crosby- Manitou State Park, and looking left you'll see a portion of the Superior National Forest. When you've filled your senses, turn around and retrace path to trailhead.

2.8 Trailhead.

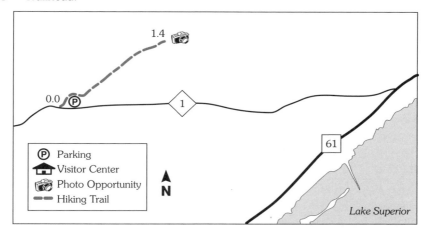

Temperance River State Park • On Highway 61, 80 miles from Duluth • *Gentle Hikes name

- **This short trail is long on delivery: beautiful canyons and waterfalls!**
- **Multiple photo ops of Lake Superior and Temperance River abound here in this unique setting.**

TRAILHEAD DIRECTIONS:
Highway 61 at mile marker 80.2, pull into paved parking area on either side of Temperance River or either side of highway. Trailhead begins from upper parking area on lake side of highway.

CONTACT:
Temperance River State Park: (218) 663-7476.

TOTAL TRAIL LENGTH, SURFACE & WIDTH:
0.2 mile; gravel and hardpacked dirt; average 3' wide. Minimal rock and root.

INCLINES & ALERTS:
No inclines greater than 10°. Steep cliff with no guardrails.

TRAILHEAD FACILITIES & FEES:
No facilities at trailhead; however, there are flush toilets (seasonal) and vault toilets in campground. Vault toilets only in picnic area on lakeside of highway. Annual or day use state park permit is required and is available at the park office.

MILEAGE & DESCRIPTION

0.0 Trailhead begins at sign indicating "Trail" from lake side of upper parking area. Ascend 19 steps (wood, no handrail, non-continuous). At intersection, turn right (left takes you to the park Visitor Center). To the right, observe many steps descending the ridge—bypass and continue straight. In a few yards, find a wooden platform with benches. This overlook view opens dramatically after leaves fall. The Superior shoreline sets a wonderful backdrop for Temperance River as it flows toward it. Several spur trails to the left lead to the campground.

As you continue, descend steps (all wood with handrails) as follows: 23, then another 4. At trail intersection, turn left to gain access to the water's edge at a pebble beach. Great photo ops here! Take time to explore the rock island. Back at trail intersection, go straight.

0.1 Past the intersection is another platform overlook (guardrails). Interesting photo ops as you look upriver.

As you continue, you will travel on a boardwalk (double handrail). At the end of the boardwalk, descend 25 steps (wood, double handrail, non-continuous). At base of steps, take the bridge (wood, double handrail) to your left. The rocks below it are a favorite spot for anglers, and you'll find the river's beauty to be prime for picture taking.

While looking toward Lake Superior, an interesting phenomenon may occur. Waves may roll in aqua blue, then suddenly turn the color of root beer as they near the shore.

After crossing the bridge, veer right at the Y and follow the trail that parallels the river's edge. Shortly, a spur trail to the right delivers another view of the Temperance River. Return to the trail. A little further along, ascend 2 steps (wood, no handrail), then continue up 29 quaint cobblestone steps (no handrail). At top of steps, turn right and cross Highway 61 bridge on the pedestrian path (guardrails). Marvelous photo op of the river plunging through steep canyons on its way to Superior. Continue to trailhead.

0.2 Trailhead.

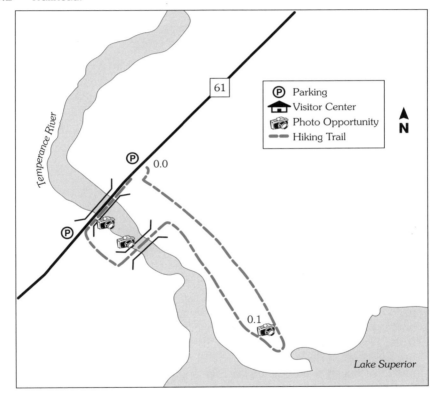

CAULDRON TRAIL

Temperance River State Park • On Highway 61, 80 miles from Duluth

- **The shortest trail in this book to showcase seven overlooks.**

- **See powerful cascades rushing through beautifully carved canyon walls, rapids engulfing rugged rock face and exquisite kettle formations!**

TRAILHEAD DIRECTIONS:
Highway 61 at mile marker 80.2, pull into paved parking area on either side of the highway or either side of Temperance River. Trailhead begins on side of highway opposite lake.

CONTACT:
Temperance River State Park: (218) 663-7476.

TOTAL TRAIL LENGTH, SURFACE & WIDTH:
0.7 mile; gravel and hardpacked dirt, but much of the trail requires hiking on basalt lava flows (large flat rock areas). Width difficult to determine because of vast, open expanses. Minimum root; moderate rock (easily negotiable bedrock, with some uneven surfaces).

INCLINES & ALERTS:
No inclines greater than 10°. Steep cliffs (no guardrail); rocks may be slippery when wet. Keep children close at hand when hiking this area.

TRAILHEAD FACILITIES & FEES:
Vault toilets in campground and picnic area—all on lake side of highway. Annual or day use state park permit is required and is available at the park office.

MILEAGE & DESCRIPTION

0.0 Trailhead begins on side of highway opposite lake at sign indicating Cauldron Trail. There are also informational kiosks about the park and SHT.

In 100', a spur trail on left leads to the river for a closer view. Continue on main trail. Fix your gaze to the left for an awesome view of Hidden Falls gorge. As you continue, notice a sign indicating "Caution—Keep children in hand." Trail surface on lava flow rock begins. Trail winds up the canyon of the Temperance River, which is wild and violent at times prior to plunging into Lake Superior. At trail intersection, a left takes you 40' to the first interpretive sign. View of waterfalls to the right and Temperance River to the left.

0.1 Ascend 11 steps (rock, no handrail). At the top, veer left up lava rock surface. In 30', ascend 15 uneven steps (stone, no handrail). In 50', find trail intersection; veer left. Once you reach the open area, take time to explore the many different views and three additional overlooks in this part of the canyon. Interpretive signs may accompany overlooks.

0.2 Do not cross the bridge. Follow sign indicating Temperance River and blue Hiking Club sign. A picnic table here provides a lovely setting for a picnic as the Temperance River serenades you. In 50', descend 6 steep but fairly even steps (stone, no handrail). These lead you to the fifth and sixth overlooks.

0.3 In this section you will find a sign on right indicating the last overlook (#7). Descend 23 steps (stone with rock wall, no handrail). Alert: This area frequently holds standing water. Waterfalls and rushing rapids through wide canyon walls make this view worth the descent. When finished exploring, turn around and retrace path to trailhead.

0.7 Trailhead

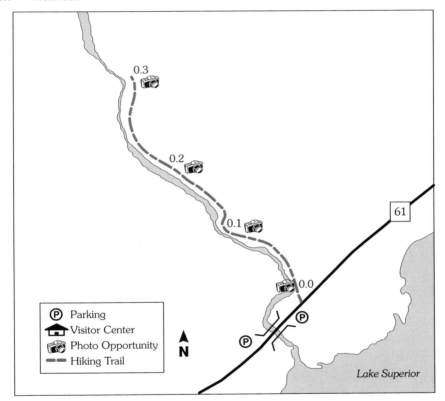

OBERG LOOP

SHT section: Oberg Mountain to Lutsen
Off Highway 61, approximately 87 miles from Duluth

- **Breathtaking vistas of Leveaux Mountain, Lake Superior, Carlton Peak, Moose Mountain and Oberg Lake—seven expansive overlooks in all!**

- **Pack a picnic lunch to enjoy from the one-of-kind, rustic log table atop Oberg Mountain.**

- **Of historical significance: This trail segment, built in 1974–1975, was the first constructed on National Forest land.**

TRAILHEAD DIRECTIONS:
Note: Turnoff from highway may be easy to miss. Highway 61 at mile marker 87.5 (watch for SHT marker on right side of highway preceding mile marker). Turn left onto Forest Road #336 (a.k.a. Onion River Road) and follow for 2.1 miles and park in gravel SHT lot on left side of road.

CONTACT:
Superior Hiking Trail: (218) 834-2700

TOTAL TRAIL LENGTH, SURFACE & WIDTH:
2.3 miles; gravel and hardpacked dirt; average 2–4' wide. Minimum to moderate rock and root.

INCLINES & ALERTS:
There are twelve inclines ranging from 12–18°. Steepest incline is 18° for 15' at 1.0 mile. Longest is 16° for 60' at 1.2 miles. Steep cliffs, many without guardrails. Depending on the season, there may be overgrowth on trail.

TRAILHEAD FACILITIES & FEES:
Vault toilet at trailhead. No fees for trail use.

MILEAGE & DESCRIPTION

0.0 Trailhead begins across Forest Road #336 at sign for Oberg Loop. Soon you should notice the sign about the North Shore Hiking Trail and another warning of sheer cliffs. A gradual ascent eventually brings you to the first intersection. Turn right following sign to Oberg Trail (left takes you on the main SHT). In just a few feet, you will find a split-log bench.

0.2 In this part of the trail, you will cross a small boardwalk, encounter occasional root and rock and continue on a gradual climb up the trail through a predominantly maple forest.

0.3 Depending on foliage, there may be numerous open views of the lake and surrounding forest areas. You will find a makeshift log bench at the base of a switchback.

0.4 At trail intersection, notice sign indicating parking area. Continue on the trail; do not turn left. You will return to this point on your way back. Shortly you will encounter sections of rocky surfaces as you begin to circle around the top of Oberg Mountain. You're on your way to the first breathtaking overlook of Leveaux Peak.

0.6 Sign for first scenic overlook. This vantage point delivers one of the most stunning views on the trail!

A flat rock surface leads to panoramic views and great photo ops of Lake Superior, Leveaux Mountain and Carlton Peak to the southwest. The Superior National Forest below spreads out like a beautiful quilt of maple, aspen, birch, cedar and spruce. A picturesque log bench makes for photo ops or a great resting spot.

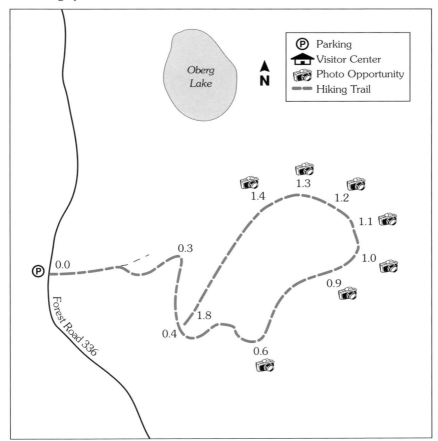

0.7 This is a relatively easy hike under the canopy of maples and birch. On your way to the next overlook, cross several sections of boardwalk.

0.9 As you continue to round Oberg Mountain, the second scenic overlook leads you to a rustic log picnic table on an immense, flat rock surface. Enjoy the view of Lake Superior and the forest below.

1.0 In this section you will encounter the area of steepest incline (18° for 15'). Soon you will come to the third scenic overlook with a dramatic view of Lake Superior from a flat, lichen- covered rock.

1.1 The fourth rocky overlook features more of Lake Superior with fabulous views of its shoreline and Sawtooth Mountains in the distance. Shortly you will descend some rocks before the trail turns away from the lake.

1.2 The fifth overlook (guardrails) showcases Moose Mountain and delivers the first of three views of Oberg Lake. Each one gets bigger and, we think, better! Keep the camera handy and definitely save some film.

From here, the trail gradually ascends toward the next overlook.

1.3 The sixth overlook features a picturesque vista of Oberg Lake nestled among evergreens. Rest for a moment on the log bench to soak up the tranquility. Great photo op, too.

1.4 En route to the final overlook, trail levels out. Cross a few sections of board-walk and one gentle incline leading up to 9 steps (wood, no handrail). The last overlook is here and it delivers—Oberg Lake, bold and beautiful!

1.8 Further along on the trail, cross a few more boardwalk sections and eventually end up back at the sign indicating parking area. This time, turn right and retrace path to trailhead. Enjoy the gentle descent back down the trail.

2.1 Back to the bench, and you're not too far from the parking area. However, take time to bask in the shade of the cedars along the way.

2.3 Trailhead.

SAYS WHO?

Still trying to kick the habit? Take a walk.

Exercise has been shown to reduce cravings for smoking.

Psychology Today [14]

Oberg Loop (see pg. 100). Photo by Melanie Morgan

Section SHT: Lutsen to Caribou Trail

Off Highway 61, approximately 90 miles from Duluth

- **See Poplar River plummet over huge boulders through a rocky ravine.**
- **Gorgeous views of Lutsen Mountain area from the parking lot!**

TRAILHEAD DIRECTIONS:

Highway 61 at mile marker 90.1 (watch for sign indicating Lutsen Mountain and Village preceding marker), turn left onto Cook County Road 5 and follow for 1.7 miles, entering Lutsen Mountain and Village. Park in Caribou Highlands lot or area for SHT on the far side of Papa Charlie's, beyond tan metal shed. Both lots are gravel.

CONTACT:

Superior Hiking Trail: (218) 834-2700

TOTAL TRAIL LENGTH, SURFACE & WIDTH:

1.7 miles; gravel and hardpacked dirt; average 9' wide, then narrows to 2–4' wide. Moderate rock and root.

INCLINES & ALERTS:

There are seven inclines, all at 12°. Steepest and longest incline is 12° for 54' at 0.7 mile. Wet areas possible. Much of this trail is shared with mountain bikers. Use caution at all turns.

TRAILHEAD FACILITIES & FEES:

Flush toilets in main chalet. No fees for trail use.

MILEAGE & DESCRIPTION

0.0 Trailhead begins on gravel road beyond Ullr Mountain chair lift and past Papa Charlie's restaurant at SHT sign. Note Moose Mountain to the left.

0.2 At trail intersection, turn left and follow sign toward Mystery Trails; listen for sounds of river as it rushes downstream.

0.3 In about 300', encounter trail intersection; veer left to follow SHT. Shortly, cross bridge (wood, double handrails) over Poplar River Falls lined with spruce, cedar and birch. Photo ops up- and downriver. Note: this bridge is closed to vehicles.

At trail intersection immediately following bridge, turn right. Watch for mountain bikers as you hike uphill. Follow gradual incline to next trail intersection.

0.5 At trail intersection, turn right and continue to follow SHT. Mountain bike trail continues to left.

0.6 Potential wet area precedes boardwalk (may be loose). There is a gradual ascent as you head toward trail switchbacks.

0.7 Area of steepest incline (12° for 54') precedes section of trail switchbacks.

0.8 At trail intersection, observe sign for overlook; veer right. As you face north, you view Poplar River as it meanders through the forest below. Turn around and retrace path to trailhead.

1.7 Trailhead.

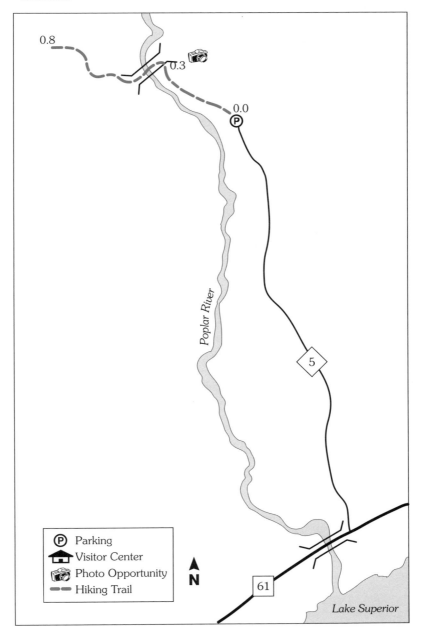

Cascade River State Park • On Highway 61, 100 miles from Duluth • *Gentle Hikes name

- **Take the shortest, easiest walk to a popular, spectacular waterfall— the Lower Cascades!**
- **Photograph the very same image featured on many postcards!**

TRAILHEAD DIRECTIONS:
Highway 61 at mile marker 99.9, pull into paved parking area opposite Cascade River Wayside.

CONTACT:
Cascade River State Park: (218) 387-1543

TOTAL TRAIL LENGTH, SURFACE & WIDTH:
0.1 mile; gravel and hardpacked dirt; average 3–4' wide.

INCLINES & ALERTS:
The only incline is 14° for 30' at 80' into trail. Although there is a guardrail at overlook, it can easily be navigated by small children. Use caution as steep cliffs follow.

TRAILHEAD FACILITIES & FEES:
No facilities available. No fees for trail use from this access point.

MILEAGE & DESCRIPTION

0.0 Trailhead begins at parking area immediately off Highway 61 (across from

Lake Superior) at Cascade River State Park kiosk (aerial view sign). Ascend 11 uneven steps (rock, no handrail, non-continuous). In 80', encounter the area of steepest incline (14° for 30'). After that, you are only 300' away from a most incredible view of the famous lower falls of the Cascade River! Bring the camera to this overlook (with guardrails) and pick your best viewing spot. Turn around and retrace path to trailhead. If you're curious as to where the rest of the trail leads, see Lower Falls Cascade River Loop pg. 110.

0.1 Trailhead.

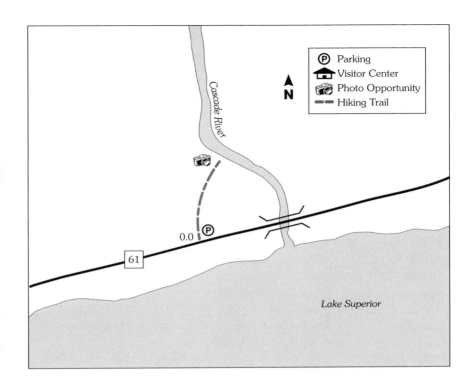

SAYS WHO?

Want to improve your relationship? Take a hike together.

Walking together improves relationships because of the time spent talking without distractions.

Health [14]

Cascade River State Park Picnic Area • On Highway 61, 100 miles from Duluth

- **This trail follows Lake Superior's shoreline while offering commanding views of the greatest of the Great Lakes!**

- **Enjoy the beautiful stands of birch while experiencing the superior sites and sounds of the lake.**

- **Sneak peeks at the boulders along the shore covered with vivid orange lichen.**

TRAILHEAD DIRECTIONS:
Highway 61 at mile marker 100.3, veer right into Cascade River State Park Picnic Area (a long pull-through section of road). Although there is no parking lot per se, parking is permitted in this area.

CONTACT:
Cascade River State Park: (218) 387-1543

TOTAL TRAIL LENGTH, SURFACE & WIDTH:
2.1 miles; grassy; average 5–6' (contingent on most recent mowing), often uneven with some holes. Minimal rock and root. Scattered areas of rock, especially under grassy areas, merit caution.

INCLINES & ALERTS:
There are two inclines ranging from 12–14°. Steepest is 14° for 10' at 1.8 miles. Unsecured logs laid to facilitate crossing some wet areas. Although this trail is basically flat, the continuous uneven surface and rocks hidden under grass earned it a rugged rating.

TRAILHEAD FACILITIES & FEES:
Vault toilet; lakeside picnic area (Cascade River State Park Picnic Area pg. 171). Annual or day use state park permit is required and is available at the park office.

MILEAGE & DESCRIPTION

0.0   Trailhead begins near vault toilet at northeast end of parking area. In a few yards, trail splits; turn left. This portion parallels the lake, serving up numerous photo ops along the way. Listen for the sounds of Superior—this is a great hike when waves are crashing!

Soon you'll enter an area shaded by many cedars, followed shortly by a nice stand of spruce.

0.2   After encountering first log crossing, look for vivid orange lichen-covered rocks near the lake.

Further down the trail you will enter a magnificent grouping of birch with a lovely canopy of maple alongside. Trail continues parallel to Lake Superior, which is known for its many moods.

0.9　At Y, veer left. To the right is Back Pack #1. This is a campsite for backpackers, so please respect the privacy of others by staying on main trail. Here trail turns away from Lake Superior and parallels Highway 61 as you enter another impressive stand of birch with a few splashes of maple. Don't forget to look across the highway for great forest views as well.

1.0　What appears to be trail's end is really an intersection. Right goes to Back Pack #1 site; left takes you across Highway 61 where the trail continues into the state park. We recommend you take neither and instead turn around and retrace path to trailhead (continuing across highway exceeds our trail length criteria).

1.8　Area of steepest incline (14° for 10').

2.1　Trailhead.

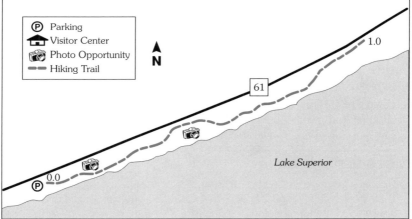

 SAYS WHO?

Want more energy? Take a hike.

Walking has been shown to increase energy levels for several hours afterwards.

Psychology Today [14]

Cascade River State Park • On Highway 61, 101 miles from Duluth • *Gentle Hikes name

- **See the cascades—a major focal point from which Cascade River State Park derived its name.**
- **This trail features some of the most frequently photographed falls and cascades along the North Shore.**

TRAILHEAD DIRECTIONS:
Highway 61 at mile marker 100.9, turn left into Cascade River State Park. Follow signs for Trail Parking, which is located about 0.8 mile from park office.

CONTACT:
Cascade River State Park: (218) 387-1543

TOTAL TRAIL LENGTH, SURFACE & WIDTH:
0.7 mile; gravel and hardpacked dirt; average 4–5' wide. Minimal rock and root.

INCLINES & ALERTS:
There is one incline of 22° for 30' at 0.4 mile. Some areas may be slippery when wet.

TRAILHEAD FACILITIES & FEES:
Vault toilet and picnic table near parking area. Annual or day use state park permit is required and is available at the park office.

MILEAGE & DESCRIPTION

0.0 Trailhead begins at far end of parking area at sign indicating "Cascade River Trail" near blue Hiking Club sign. In this section you will ascend and descend 14 steps (wood, handrail) before arriving at a Y in trail; continue straight. Ascend 16 uneven steps (stone, no handrail), then descend 16 steps (wood, handrail).

0.1 This brings you to a trail intersection. Cross Cascade River over bridge (wood, double handrail). Pause while crossing bridge for beautiful views upriver of cascades and downriver toward Lake Superior. Immediately after bridge, descend 12 steps (stone, handrail) for a spectacular overlook; postcard quality photo op of cascades! Back at end of bridge, take the trail closest to the river that leads toward Lake Superior. In this section, descend 47 steps (wood, some handrail, non-continuous). This brings you to an overlook (guardrails) and a photo op from a vantage point looking over the falls.

0.2 Down 34 platform-type steps (wood, double handrail, non-continuous) to another postcard quality photo op—the impressive Lower Cascade falls! The trails behind you lead to Cascade Lodge and Highway 61 parking area. Continue straight on main trail following the river and descend 53 steps (wood, no handrail, non-continuous) to base of river.

0.3 During the summer, a lovely fern glade grows here. Take some time to explore this area where the river empties into Lake Superior. Then ascend 15 steps (wood, double handrail) toward highway, turn left and continue across the bridge (pedestrian lane with guardrails) over Cascade River. Photo ops abound. At end of bridge, turn left and ascend 20 uneven steps (stone, no handrail) to kiosk (state trail aerial view map marker). Small overlook here, then ascend 10 steps (stone, no handrail).

0.4 Continue straight on trail (paths to the right lead to campground). Further along, you will encounter a decline and the area of steepest incline (22° for 30') before coming to a small spur to the left. This spur brings you to a bench and a foliage-dependent view of Highway 61 bridge and Lake Superior. Back on the trail, ascend 4 steps (wood, no handrail) and continue to another overlook (guardrail) above the river. Ascend an additional 19 steps (stone, no handrail, non-continuous) and yet another overlook (guardrail). Shortly, ascend 3 steps (stone, no handrail), then 21 steps (wood, no handrail). This brings you back to the intersection with bridge. Turn right and retrace path to trailhead.

0.7 Trailhead.

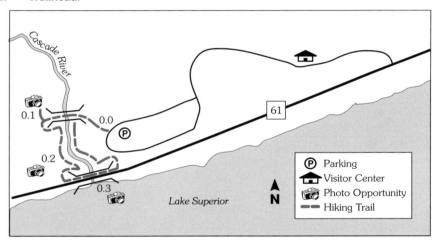

SHT Section: Cascade River to Bally Creek Road
Off Highway 61, approximately 101 miles from Duluth

- **Hike along the upper region of the Cascade River as it tumbles and falls over rocks and boulders.**
- **Experience the majesty of some very old cedars.**
- **Challenge yourself to find Hidden Falls.**

TRAILHEAD DIRECTIONS:
Highway 61 at mile marker 101.7, turn left onto Cook County Road 7 and follow for 1.0 mile. Veer left onto County Road 44 and follow for 0.5 mile to stop sign. Turn left onto County Road 45 and follow for 2.5 miles to SHT gravel parking area (just beyond small green Pike Lake Road 731 sign).

CONTACT:
Superior Hiking Trail: (218) 834-2700

TOTAL TRAIL LENGTH, SURFACE & WIDTH:
0.8 mile; hardpacked dirt and gravel; average 1–4' wide. Significant root, moderate rock. Several boardwalk paths.

INCLINES & ALERTS:
There are four inclines ranging from 12–22°. Steepest incline is 22° for 10' at 0.2 mile. Some boardwalk path may be uneven, broken or unsecured. Possible wet areas from runoff. Trail has indistinct turnaround point (see description below at 0.4 miles).

TRAILHEAD FACILITIES & FEES:
No facilities available. No fees for trail use.

MILEAGE & DESCRIPTION

0.0   Trailhead begins at lower end of parking area at SHT sign. Listen for the Cascade River as the trail runs parallel to it. Alert: After walking under the overpass, the next 300' contains numerous boardwalk sections (some loose and/or broken) with moderate rock and root.

0.1   Old cedars line the trail. Although quite majestic, they pose a significant root surface to be carefully negotiated (a few rocks interspersed). In 70', find additional boardwalk sections followed by more uneven root surface.

0.2   Area of steepest incline (22° for 10'). Alert: This section contains numerous boardwalk sections (some loose and/or broken) interspersed with significant exposed tree roots. Descend 7 steps (wood, no handrail) followed by a section of boardwalk. Then ascend 3 steps (wood, no handrail), cross another section of boardwalk and descend 3 steps (wood, no handrail). If this area is soggy you might find animal tracks.

More boardwalk before the trail ascends, then descends steeply along a heavily rooted area.

0.4 Clues to Hidden Falls location:

#1 Find a small SHT sign (above *eye* level) on a tree to your right.

#2 About 80' further, locate an area where you can step down to the river rock (if water levels are too high, abort search).

#3 Locate a cliff face on the opposite side of the river between washouts.

#4 Observe kettles of various sizes formed in softer rock birthed by the churning waters of spring runoff. Depending on the river level, you may be able to locate Hidden Falls in this area. Happy searching! At this point, turn around and retrace path to trailhead.

0.8 Trailhead.

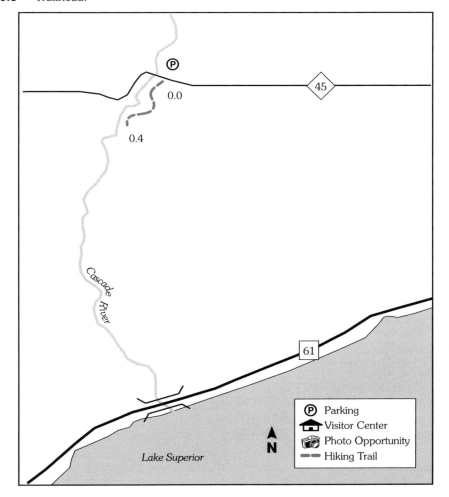

Pincushion Mtn. Cross-Country Ski Trails • Off Highway 61, approximately 109 miles from Duluth

- **Spectacular aerial view of Grand Marais harbor and Artists' Point, similar to those which can be seen from Pincushion Mountain Overlook (pg. 156). However, this trail's end affords you a nearly 270° view including Pincushion Mountain, Lake Superior and part of the Sawtooth range.**
- **Check out this trail in winter for an awesome snowshoeing adventure!**

TRAILHEAD DIRECTIONS:
Highway 61 at mile marker 109.4 in Grand Marais, turn left onto the Gunflint Trail (County Road 12) and follow for 2 miles. Turn right onto Pincushion Drive (County Road 53) and follow for 0.1 mile to overlook.

CONTACT:
Pincushion Mountain B&B: (218) 387-1276

TOTAL TRAIL LENGTH, SURFACE & WIDTH:
0.5 mile; hardpacked gravel, grass; average 8' wide.

INCLINES & ALERTS:
There is only one incline: 18° for 15', and begins at approach to trailhead as a decline. Approach to trailhead has a gravel decline (18° for 15'). After heavy rains, runoff area on trail may contain water; no footbridge. Steep dropoff (no guardrails) near overlook.

TRAILHEAD FACILITIES & FEES:
Vault toilet (wheelchair accessible). No fees for trail use during non-ski season.

MILEAGE & DESCRIPTION

0.0 Trailhead begins opposite entrance to parking area. Take gravel trail toward two large rocks and sign indicating "No Motorized Vehicles." In 60', you will cross a runoff area (after heavy rain, there may be some water here; no footbridge).

Shortly, a trail will enter from the left. Continue straight on gravel path through spruce, birch and aspen.

0.1 At Y continue straight and follow sign that indicates "Snowshoe Trail;" this leads to overlook.

0.2 Overlook from broad, open, flat rock area. Almost like standing on a mountaintop in that you can see so much from such a little point! After you have experienced this expansive scene, turn around and retrace path to trailhead.

0.5 Trailhead

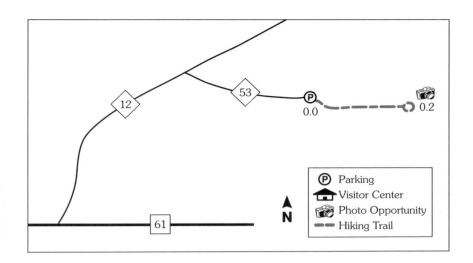

 Foot Note:

Pincushion Mountain hosts several cross-country ski trails and a B&B. They offer cross-country ski lessons for all levels (218-387-1276 or visit www.pincushionbb.com).

 SAYS WHO?

Do you have high blood pressure?

Physical activity such as walking can reduce and prevent high blood pressure.

Preventive Medicine [27]

Grand Marais Public Water Access (a.k.a. Boulder Park) • Off Highway 61, 109 miles from Duluth
*Gentle Hikes name

- **Take in the beauty of Lake Superior and Grand Marais Harbor, almost simultaneously!**
- **A great place to see a variety of waterfowl.**
- **This hike provides a very attractive view of the Lighthouse and Sawtooth Mountains silhouetted against the lake.**

TRAILHEAD DIRECTIONS:
Highway 61 at mile marker 109.8, turn right onto Broadway Avenue and follow 0.3 mile to public water access (this is also a wayside, see Grand Marais Public Water Access pg. 156).

CONTACT:
Grand Marais Area Chamber of Commerce: (218) 387-1400

TOTAL TRAIL LENGTH, SURFACE & WIDTH:
0.7 mile; gravel, cement sea wall, intermittent rock (basically flat); average 4' wide. Minimal rock and root.

INCLINES & ALERTS:
No inclines greater than 10°. Natural rock formation steps may necessitate careful negotiation. Some rock surfaces are uneven and all rock is slippery when wet.

TRAILHEAD FACILITIES & FEES:
Portable toilets (seasonal); several picnic tables (one with extension), benches, boat launch. No fees for trail use.

MILEAGE & DESCRIPTION

0.0 Trail begins near the left side of Coast Guard Station where paved parking lot ends and wide gravel driveway begins. In 200', ascend 3 steps (stone, no handrail) turning right onto cement sea wall.

0.1 Rock surface begins (fairly flat and level), yielding to cement sea wall (cable railing). Ascend 4 steps; sea wall continues (no handrail). You will also encounter natural rock formation steps in this section, which may be uneven.

0.2 Sea wall (cable rail) remains fairly constant with occasional interruptions of rock surfaces. Various waterfowl frequent this area.

0.3 Lighthouse and foghorn with Sawtooth Mountains in the distance. Turn around and retrace path to trailhead. Enjoy lovely views of Artists' Point on the return.

0.7 Trailhead.

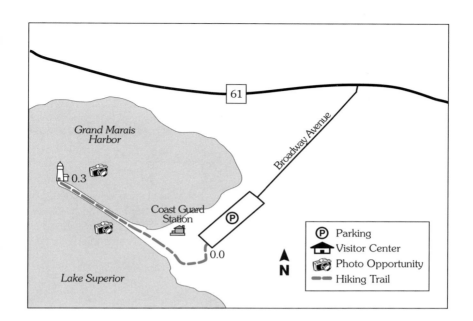

Joint pain keeping you off the trail?

Jarring forces on knees and other joints can be reduced 12-25% by using hiking poles.

Harvard Women's Health Watch [28]

SHT section: Cook County Road 58 to Kadunce River
Off Highway 61, approximately 113 miles from Duluth

- **This trail features the deepest gorge in Minnesota, which is located above the Devil Track River!**
- **Turn up your nose (in a good way); this trail offers abundant pine stands.**
- **Hike through a 1937 pine plantation.**

TRAILHEAD DIRECTIONS:
Highway 61 at mile marker 113.7 (watch for sign indicating Cook County Road 58 after crossing Devil Track River), turn left onto County Road 58 and veer to the right uphill for 0.2 mile. At Y in road, veer left onto Lindskog Road and follow for 0.6 mile to gravel parking lot on left for Superior Hiking Trail.

CONTACT:
Superior Hiking Trail: (218) 834-2700

TOTAL TRAIL LENGTH, SURFACE & WIDTH:
2 miles; hardpacked dirt and gravel; average 1–3' wide. Minimum rock; moderate root in sections.

INCLINES & ALERTS:
There are ten inclines ranging from 18–22° (most occur after 0.5 mile into trail). Steepest and longest is 22° for 84' at 1.0 mile. Overlooks have no guard rails. Erosion and steep cliffs at various sections of trail.

TRAILHEAD FACILITIES & FEES:
No facilities available. No fees for trail use.

MILEAGE & DESCRIPTION

0.0 Trailhead begins at lower end of parking lot near wooden SHT sign (no notation for Barrier Falls Overlook; follow sign for Grand Marais Overlook). Immediately you will hear the sounds of Wood's Creek as trail parallels it for the first 100'. Descend 7 steps (wood, no handrail). In 300', cross creek over footbridge (wood, no handrail). Travel through a nice stand of birch.

0.2 Depending on foliage, views of canyon may be visible. Listen for rushing water in the canyon below. Pass through a larger area of birch and pine, which serves as a prelude to a majestic stand of tall pine.

0.3 Descend 7 steps (wood, no handrail). Shortly you will find a spur trail to cliff (no guardrail) and view of river. In 75', walk around boardwalk (at time of writing, these timbers were rotted). Enter another section of towering pine as trail winds through densely shaded area along ridge.

0.4 Cross bridge (wood, double handrail) over picturesque, miniature gorge lined with volcanic rock walls and flowing cascades. In 200', ascend 26 uneven steps (wood, no handrail) into another impressive stand of pine with spruce and fir. Take a deep breath—the fragrance is refreshing!

0.6 Ascend 15 steps (wood, no handrail). Forest soon changes to aspen; however, pine will dominate again, eventually leading to a mixed forest.

1.0 Natural overlook (no guardrail) of river canyon walls before descending steep grade (22° for 84') with loose gravel toward Barrier Falls Overlook. On a clear day, you can see Lake Superior in the distance. At base of decline, find another view of the river carving its way through steep canyon walls. Ascend a moderately rooted incline leading to a nice view of the gorge, which puts its depth into perspective. Catch a glimpse of Barrier Falls. Turn around at sign indicating Barrier Falls and retrace path to trailhead.

2.0 Trailhead.

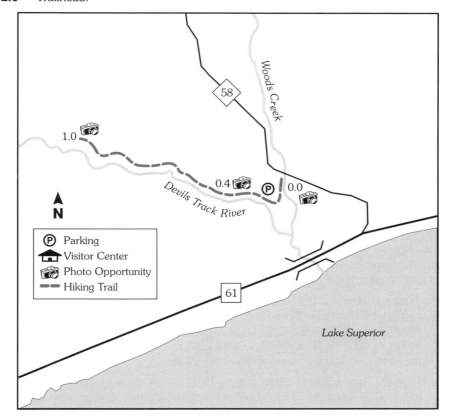

SHT Section: Kadunce River to Judge C.R. Magney State Park

On Highway 61, 119 miles from Duluth

- **An incredibly scenic hike offering many breathtaking views into the depths of the river's gorge.**
- **Trail follows Kadunce River in a beautifully wooded setting for the first 0.1 mile.**
- **This river is also a designated trout stream.**

TRAILHEAD DIRECTIONS:
Highway 61 at mile marker 118.9, after crossing bridge, turn right into Kadunce River Wayside paved parking lot (highway sign is spelled Kodonce Creek).

CONTACT:
Superior Hiking Trail: (218) 834-2700

TOTAL TRAIL LENGTH, SURFACE & WIDTH:
1.2 miles; gravel and hardpacked dirt; average 3' wide. Moderate root, minimum rock.

INCLINES & ALERTS:
There is one incline of 16° for 20' at 0.2 mile. You will need to cross Highway 61 to locate trailhead. Natural overlooks with erosion beneath. Steep cliffs in various trail sections with no guardrails.

TRAILHEAD FACILITIES & FEES:
Picnic table with pavement extending to it. See Kadunce River Wayside (pg. 158). No fees for trail use.

MILEAGE & DESCRIPTION

0.0 Trailhead begins at SHT sign indicating Kadunce bridge. It is located across Highway 61 from Kadunce River Wayside. Enter through a beautifully shaded forest as the trail meanders along the Kadunce River. Miniature waterfall basins serve as home to various species of trout. Within the first 500', several spur trails beckon a closer walk to river's edge.

0.1 As trail begins to climb gently, notice the moss and lichen-covered rhyolite cliff walls. Ascend 40 steps (wood, no handrail). At top of steps, veer left (to the right is a spur trail that is closed). Shortly you will find a natural overlook (no guardrail) as the Kadunce rounds a bend. See if you can locate the swirl cave tucked in beneath cedar and spruce.

0.2 At trail intersection, turn right (however, if you like adventure, take the spur to the left and have fun carefully exploring this lush forest that takes you to river's edge. Alert: Erosion near cliff edge). In 100', ascend area of steepest incline (16° for 20').

Shortly, an SHT Spur Trail sign serves as a trail marker. Views of river gorge abound! To get a perspective on tree height, look down into the canyon and find a tree with its roots in the river bed.

0.3 At Y, trail splits and reconnects in approximately 400'. Trail to the left parallels river gorge while trail to the right goes through the woods. However, path along the river gorge shows two more swirl caves nestled in the canyon wall.

After trail reconnects, it eventually leads to river's edge.

0.6 Bridge (wood, double handrail) over Kadunce River. Lovely views up- and downriver of gently tumbling cascades. Turn around here and retrace path to trailhead.

1.2 Trailhead.

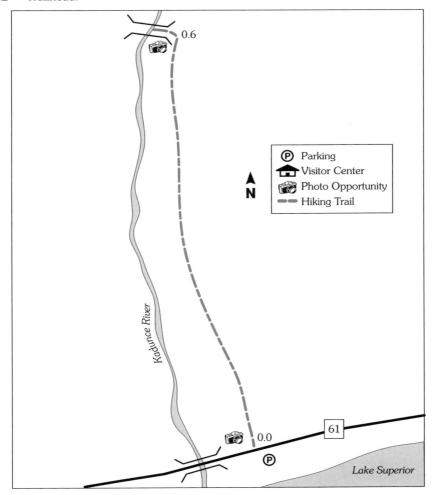

BRULE RIVER LOOP*

Judge C.R. Magney State Park • On Highway 61, 124 miles from Duluth • *Gentle Hikes name

- **Impressive views of the Brule River!**
- **This state park is named in honor of C. R. Magney who was instrumental in the establishment of numerous parks on the North Shore.**
- **Wide variety of wildflowers during the summer on optional spur trail.**

TRAILHEAD DIRECTIONS:
Highway 61 at mile marker 124, turn left into Judge C.R. Magney State Park. Follow signs indicating Trail Parking (0.2 mile from park office). Trailhead is located immediately to the right as you enter gravel parking area. Start at sign indicating Devil's Kettle Trail.

CONTACT:
Judge C.R. Magney State Park: (218) 387-3039.

TOTAL TRAIL LENGTH, SURFACE & WIDTH:
0.4 mile (*optional spur adds additional 0.4 mile); hardpacked dirt; average 2–3' wide (narrower for optional spur). Minimum rock and root.

INCLINES & ALERTS:
No inclines greater than 10°. Optional spur trail may have significant vegetation overgrowth.

TRAILHEAD FACILITIES & FEES:
Vault toilet, water (seasonal), picnic tables. Annual or day use state park permit is required and is available at the park office.

MILEAGE & DESCRIPTION

0.0 Trailhead begins at sign indicating Devil's Kettle Trail; soon you will cross a bridge (wood, double handrail). Follow path to monument honoring Judge C. R. Magney (off to the left). A bridge (cement, green handrails) takes you across the Brule River with marvelous photo ops of up and down stream!

0.1 After crossing bridge, veer right and follow trail along river (a left leads to Devil's Kettle Trail, which exceeded book criteria). However, in front of you is a wonderful little picnic area in a nice wooded setting. If you didn't bring a lunch, it's still a great place to relax.

At Y in trail, veer right and continue past steps (if you do venture down, there are 17 steps (wood, handrail). You'll get a closer look at the river and maybe even see some waterfowl. We found mergansers to be very active near here. There are also beautiful views of the Brule and some small falls. (Alert: No guardrails; tree roots and erosion).

0.2 At next Y, veer right (paths reconnect, but views are better this way) through a lovely fir grove as trail continues along river toward Highway 61. There are several paths in this area that lead to the highway; however, we found the best by turning left at the next trail intersection, then taking a right. You'll see (and hear) the highway. At guardrail, take another right, which leads you across a bridge (cement, double guardrail) running parallel to Highway 61. This is another great place for photo ops of the Brule. Look across the highway for views of Lake Superior and the historic Naniboujou Lodge, which is open for both lodging and fine dining.

At end of bridge, turn right and descend 17 steps (wood, no handrail).

0.3 At trail intersection, turn right for option* or continue straight and return to monument via path through wooded area along river. At monument, continue toward trailhead.

0.4 Trailhead

*Option: At trail intersection, hike may be lengthened by turning right and taking the optional spur trail, which narrows as it runs along the Brule River toward Lake Superior. You'll find numerous photo ops along this section. This is a great trail for viewing a variety of wildflowers (bring the zoom lens). Follow it for 0.2 mile to a place where trail opens up and river meets breakwater. We recommend stopping here because excessive overgrowth, very low tree branches and rooted surfaces lie beyond this point. Turn around and retrace path back to intersection.

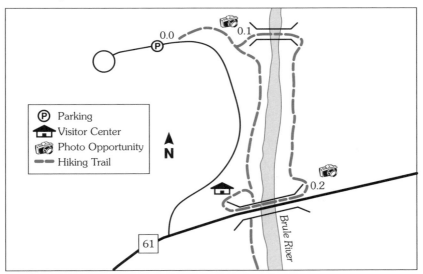

The Naniboujou Lodge is listed in the National Register of Historical Places and is one of the "must-see" locations along the North Shore (218-387-2688 or www.naniboujou.com).

SHT Section: Judge C.R. Magney State Park to Arrowhead Trail
On Highway 61, 124 miles from Duluth

- **One of the most gentle sections of the Superior Hiking Trail on a gradual ascent.**
- **Hike on a wide trail through a mixed forest to Gauthier Creek.**

TRAILHEAD DIRECTIONS:
Highway 61 at mile marker 124, turn left into Judge C.R. Magney State Park. Follow signs indicating Trail Parking for 0.2 mile from park office. Trailhead begins at far end of gravel parking lot in loop area.

CONTACT:
Superior Hiking Trail: (218) 834-2700

TOTAL TRAIL LENGTH, SURFACE & WIDTH:
1.7 miles; hardpacked dirt, grass, loose gravel; average 6' wide. Minimum rock and root.

INCLINES & ALERTS:
No inclines greater than 10°. Grassy surface can be uneven in places.

TRAILHEAD FACILITIES & FEES:
Vault toilet, water (seasonal), picnic tables. Annual or day use state park permit is required and is available at the park office.

MILEAGE & DESCRIPTION

0.0 Trailhead begins at far end of parking lot in loop area near SHT sign. In a few yards, you will find a larger SHT sign with park map attached. Turn left following sign indicating Gauthier Creek.

0.1 A stand of fir and spruce brings you to first trail intersection; turn right following SHT logo. A gradual ascent leads you through a mixed forest.

0.4 Bench in wooded setting. Great place to stop and enjoy the beauty of the forest.

0.8 At Y, sign indicates SHT to left; veer right to Gauthier Creek.

0.9 Gauthier Creek; turn around and retrace path to beginning of trailhead. Enjoy the gentle descent back.

1.7 Trailhead.

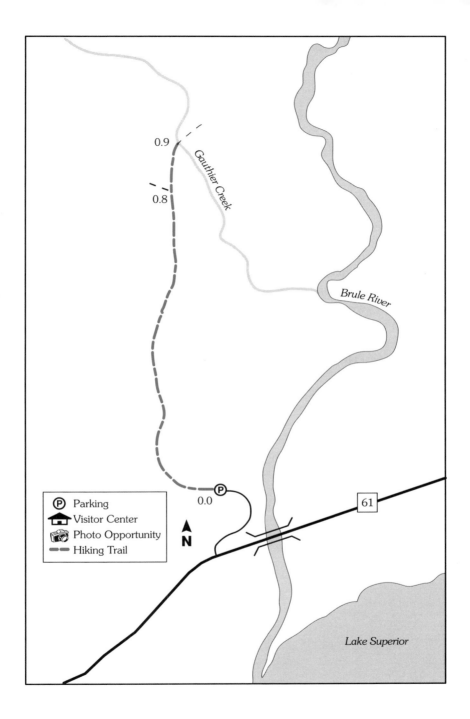

0.9

Gauthier Creek

0.8

Brule River

P Parking
Visitor Center
Photo Opportunity
Hiking Trail

0.0

N

61

Lake Superior

WEBSTER-ASHBURTON TRAIL & PICNIC AREA*

Grand Portage State Park • On Highway 61, 150 miles from Duluth • *Gentle Hikes name

- **Wonderfully wooded, off-the-beaten-path picnic sites with fabulous views of the Pigeon River.**
- **Site of the Webster-Ashburton Treaty of 1842 between the U.S. and Canada, which determined where national boundaries would be drawn.**

TRAILHEAD DIRECTIONS:
Highway 61 at mile marker 150.6, turn left into Grand Portage State Park (if you miss it, you'll be turning around at customs at the Canadian border!). Parking is located at park entrance.

TOTAL TRAIL LENGTH, SURFACE & WIDTH:
0.4 mile; paved; average 8' wide, for first 0.2 mile. Grass and hardpacked dirt; average 1–6' wide. Minimal rock and root.

INCLINES & ALERTS:
No inclines greater than 10°. No drinking fountains available. Bring your own water! Steep cliffs beyond picnic area (no guardrails).

TRAILHEAD FACILITIES & FEES:
Visitor Center and gift shop, vault toilet (all wheelchair accessible). Annual or day use state park permit is required and is available at the park office.

MILEAGE & DESCRIPTION

0.0   Trailhead begins across from Visitor Center at sign indicating picnic area. This trail is unique in that it also hosts a wonderful picnic site (Grand Portage State Park Picnic Area pg. 174) with views of the Pigeon River as it flows through a mixed forest. There are three picnic sites along this trail.

0.2   Pavement ends. Shortly you will encounter a bridge (handrails). Alert: Steep cliffs with no guardrails on riverside. Historical marker just 18' ahead. Take time to read about this interesting treaty that determined national boundaries. Retrace path to trailhead.

0.4   Trailhead.

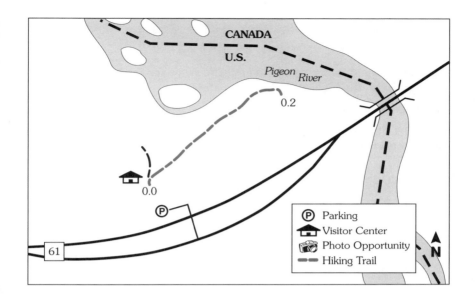

Have trouble drinking enough? (Water, that is!)

Studies show that some people have an easier time drinking sports drinks than water during physical activity because sports drinks taste good.

Appetite [29]

Grand Portage State Park • On Highway 61, 150 miles from Duluth

- **Angular, rugged rock face sets a majestic stage for the center attraction of High Falls—the highest in the entire state!**
- **See approximately 3,200 gallons of water per second pouring over the falls.**
- **View the remains of an 1899 log flume built to circumvent timber from the trip over the falls.**

TRAILHEAD DIRECTIONS:
Highway 61 at mile marker 150.6, turn left into Grand Portage State Park (if you miss it, you'll be turning around at customs at the Canadian border!). Paved parking is located at park entrance.

TOTAL TRAIL LENGTH, SURFACE & WIDTH:
1.0 mile; paved; average 8' wide and constructed to meet the standards for Universal Design.

INCLINES & ALERTS:
No inclines greater than 10°. No drinking water available. Bring your own water.

TRAILHEAD FACILITIES & FEES:
Visitor Center and gift shop, vault toilet (all wheelchair accessible). Annual or day use state park permit is required and is available at the park office.

MILEAGE & DESCRIPTION

0.0 Trailhead begins at Visitor Center on paved pathway. Notice the lovely views
 of the Pigeon River through a mixed forest.

There are a total of nine benches strategically placed approximately every 400' along the trail (pavement extends to bench).

0.4 Vault toilet to the left. Soon the boardwalk begins (double handrail), which leads to three different options for viewing the falls (two have stairs, one does not).

0.5 Trail intersection.

 Option #1. Veer left and ascend 40 steps (wood, double handrail, non-continuous) that lead to the first viewing platform equipped with bench and guardrails. This vantage point offers a phenomenal view of the thundering falls. We stood in awe...simply put, words cannot do justice.

Notice the trail across the river; look closer and you will see the remains of an 1899 log flume. To the east, on a clear day, look for Isle Royale and Pigeon Point in the distance.

The other two viewing areas can be accessed from the base of the steps by staying on the boardwalk.

Option #2. The middle viewing area affords a spectacular falls view and is located on the boardwalk itself (no steps).

Option #3. The upper observation deck can be accessed by ascending 17 steps (wood, double handrail). The falls are mesmerizing and clearly the main event. Look downstream for an eye-catching view of the vivid orange lichen that covers sections of the canyon walls above the Pigeon River.

Retrace path to trailhead.

1.0   Trailhead.

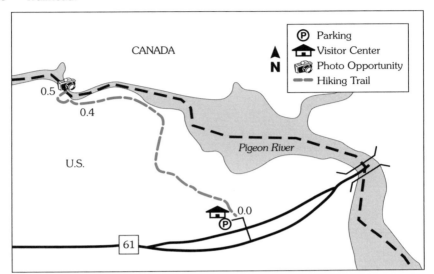

 SAYS WHO?

Hiking + soda pop = discomfort!

Soft drinks are not recommended as a fluid replacement because of their concentrated sugars, carbonation, and/or caffeine contents. Carbonation takes up space in the stomach that could be used by additional fluids. And caffeine causes you to lose more fluid than contained in the drink itself!

Nutrition: Concepts and Controversies [30]

ALMOST HIKES
An Almost Hike is:
-a very short trail, ranging from 100' to 0.6 mile with spectacular scenery!

-typically not a trail per se, but a route to scenic beauty.

-usually has an original name as this concept is original to our book.

We hope you'll enjoy the following strolls scattered from Duluth all the way to Grand Marais. We give you highlights, total length/surface, safety concerns, amenities, applicable fees and a brief narrative of what you'll see while there.

Most Almost Hikes are very suitable for families travelling with small children. Great leg stretchers and highly scenic—but please heed safety concerns.

Brule River (see pg. 122). Photo by Ladona Tornabene

CANAL PARK LIGHTHOUSE STROLL*

Duluth, MN • *Gentle Hikes name

- **Fabulous views of Duluth's 'City on a Hill' as well as a commanding view of the world famous Aerial Lift Bridge and, of course, Lake Superior!**

- **This is the best place to watch ships up close. Announcements are often made concerning specifics about the ships as they pass through the shipping lane.**

DIRECTIONS:

From Interstate 35 North, exit at Lake Avenue South; turn right onto Canal Park Drive and follow to parking area of choice (wheelchair accessible spaces).

TOTAL TRAIL LENGTH & SURFACE:

0.4 mile; paved with ramp access. Flat with the exception of 15 steps (cement, double handrail) leading up to actual lighthouse.

ALERT:

This is a multi-use, non-motorized path.

AMENITIES:

Flush toilets available in Lake Superior Maritime Visitor Center. No fees for trail use; however, there may be a fee for parking.

NARRATIVE:

Trailhead begins and ends at Lake Superior Maritime Visitor Center (open year-round, mid-December through mid-March, Friday–Sunday only). Plan to spend some time in there as it houses several exhibits and programs on maritime history and their connection to the Corps of Engineers. The stroll out toward the lighthouse is on a very level cement. Photo ops abound.

LEIF ERIKSON ROSE GARDEN

Duluth, MN

- **Some 40,000 roses!**

- **See winners of All-American Rose Selections on display. Peak blooming is mid-July to late August.**

- **Italian-style gazebo, authentic fountain and herb garden, all set with a backdrop of Lake Superior and Duluth's most famous landmark—the Aerial Lift Bridge.**

DIRECTIONS:

Interstate 35 North at Lake Avenue exit, turn left. Turn right at the first traffic light onto Superior Street. At 10th Avenue E, turn right onto London Road (this is where London Road begins and then runs parallel to Superior Street). Drive to paved parking lot on right side of street between S 13th Avenue E and S 14th Avenue E.

TOTAL TRAIL LENGTH & SURFACE:
0.2 mile around perimeter (will vary depending upon how explored); brick cobblestone and cement. Grassy surfaces offer up-close view of roses.

ALERT:
No pets allowed in Rose Garden, please. It is illegal to pick roses. With over 70,000 visitors per year, there would be no Rose Garden if everyone picked roses.

AMENITIES:
Flush toilets and water fountain (all seasonal) available near parking lot; benches. No fees for trail use.

NARRATIVE:
Trailhead begins at parking lot on path that circles around the rose garden. The first half is brick cobblestone yielding to a wide cement path, including the sidewalk along London Road. To give the olfactory glands a workout, you'll want to venture off the path onto the grass to access the four circles of rose bushes. Strategically placed benches throughout offer ample resting and viewing places.

There are four informational markers placed around the rose garden. They are packed with information such as the intriguing history of the Rose Garden (which was established September 6, 1967 by the Duluth Rose Society), the most frequently asked questions, fascinating facts about All-American Rose Selections and tips on how to grow beautiful roses.

The lovely Italian-style gazebo is often used as a site for wedding pictures, but makes for great photo ops whatever the occasion! In the center of the largest rose circle stands a fountain with a history. It was built in 1905 and was used for watering horses (and dogs, too—notice lapping bowl at base) until the automobile rumbled onto the scene, relegating the fountain to its present ornamental state.

Note: In mid-October, when the roses are put to bed, the remaining blooms are cut and distributed to anyone who is visiting at the time.

ROCK POND
Bagley Nature Area • University of Minnesota Duluth

- **Take some time (and photo ops) to explore the reflective beauty of the forest—complements of Rock Pond. Although lovely in summer, it's simply stunning in autumn.**

- **There are also some eye-catching crabapple trees here that produce in abundance during the summer.**

DIRECTIONS:
Interstate 35 North at exit 258 (watch for sign indicating University of Minnesota Duluth), turn left at the end of exit ramp. Continue up 21st Avenue East until it ends at Woodland. Turn right and follow for 0.9 mile to St. Marie Street (traffic light and gas stations on the corner). Turn left and follow for 0.5

mile to one block beyond Montrose Avenue. Turn right into parking lot (watch for sign indicating Bagley Nature Area). Note: If parking during September to May, see Alert section below.

TOTAL TRAIL LENGTH & SURFACE:
0.1 mile; grass, mulch over hardpacked dirt.

ALERT:
Parking is limited in this lot to the few meters near trailhead during September through May. Additional parking in pay lot located on University Drive.

AMENITIES & FEES:
No amenities. No fees for trail use; however, from September through May, there is a fee for parking (unless you are fortunate enough to find street parking that is not in a residential zone).

NARRATIVE:
Trailhead begins near metered parking area. You will see a kiosk with map display. Enter trail by yellow gate. Immediately experience the tranquility of Rock Pond as you travel through an open area. Soon you will be amid mountain ash, birch and maple on a frequently mulched trail. At first intersection turn left; at next intersection turn left again following along Rock Pond through a stand of pine. At Y, take path to the left. It will bring you to the parking area. Note: hike does not loop completely around pond.

TWO RIVERS VIEW*

Lester Park • Duluth, MN • *Gentle Hikes name

• **Incredible vantage point for viewing Lester River and Amity Creek.**

DIRECTIONS:
Interstate 35 North to end; at split veer left (do not follow North Shore). Cross London Road and begin up 26th Avenue E, turning right onto Superior Street. At intersection of Superior Street and Lester River Road (approximately 61st Avenue E), turn left onto Lester River Road. Paved parking lot is immediately on the left.

TOTAL TRAIL LENGTH & SURFACE:
0.4 mile; gravel, cement (part of it is on sidewalk).

ALERT:
Sidewalk for viewing area runs parallel to Superior Street.

AMENITIES & FEES:
Flush toilets (seasonal; not wheelchair accessible as of 12/01), covered picnic tables, playground. No fees for trail use.

NARRATIVE:
Trailhead begins on a gravel path located at end of parking lot closest to Superior Street, in an open area heading toward restroom building. It travels along the Lester River until ending at sidewalk parallel to Superior Street. Turn

right onto sidewalk and follow until reaching views of the Lester River and Amity Creek, which are set amid trees and a quaint bridge within the park. This vantage point has a reputation for attracting many shutterbugs!

BREAKWATER LIGHTHOUSE POINT STROLL*

Off Highway 61, 26 miles from Duluth • *Gentle Hikes name

- **One of the few places on the shore to showcase a nearly 360° sweep of Lake Superior.**
- **Terrific views of ore docks and city of Two Harbors. Look closely to spot a lone tug called** *The Edna G.*
- **Magnificent view of the old Two Harbors Lighthouse nestled among a forest of birch and spruce.**

DIRECTIONS:
Highway 61 at mile marker 26 (Note: You will not find actual mile marker—use odometer reading from marker 25), turn right onto Waterfront Drive (corner of Dairy Queen and Blackwoods Restaurant) and follow for 0.5 mile to South Avenue. Turn left and follow for 0.3 mile to 3rd Street; turn right and follow for 0.2 mile to paved parking area (ample spaces for RVs).

TOTAL TRAIL LENGTH & SURFACE:
0.6 mile; paved with access ramp.

ALERT:
No railing on one side of breakwater walkway.

AMENITIES & FEES:
Portable toilets (seasonal), picnic tables, boat launch, small gift shop in lighthouse. No fees for trail use.

NARRATIVE:
Trailhead begins at far end of parking area facing the lake. Descend 10 steps (cement, double handrail) or take the alternative paved ramp toward fog horn/light. A cable railing has been placed on one side of the 8' wide concrete walkway. Follow the breakwater path 0.3 mile to the end. After enjoying the above highlights, turn around and retrace the walkway to trailhead. This area also features a wayside (pg. 149)

 Foot Note:

Two Harbors breakwater was constructed between 1947–51 by the U.S. Army Corps of Engineers.

IONA'S BEACH

On Highway 61, 42 miles from Duluth

- **A thick stand of pine lines the path to a rhyolite pebble beach.**
- **The rare beach of rhyolite shingles, which were worn away from nearby cliffs, make a musical noise if the waves hit them just right.**
- **When completed, this will be a safe harbor area for small watercraft to take temporary refuge from storms.**

DIRECTIONS:
Highway 61 at mile marker 42, turn right into parking area (gravel, but will be paved when complete).

TOTAL TRAIL LENGTH & SURFACE:
0.2 mile (varies depending on how explored); asphalt, hardpacked dirt, gravel and grass.

ALERT:
Depending on how area is explored, steep cliffs and overgrowth in places.

AMENITIES & FEES:
No amenities as of 12/01. No fees for trail use.

NARRATIVE:
Trailhead begins at the northeast end of parking area near a marvelous stand of pine, balsam fir, birch and alder. At the intersection, take time to read the informational display. Then follow the various spur trails. The left leads to rhyolite pebble beach; the middle to a rocky promontory; the right to a large, rocky side of beach that goes down to water's edge.

PEBBLE BEACH

Split Rock Lighthouse State Park • On Highway 61, 46 miles from Duluth

- **Extraordinary, classic views of Split Rock Lighthouse and Piney Island.**
- **Remnants of an early fishing village may be visible beneath Superior's surface.**

DIRECTIONS:
Highway 61 at mile marker 45.9, turn right into Split Rock Lighthouse State Park. Follow past Visitor Center, turning right onto the first street you encounter. Follow for 0.5 mile to paved parking lot (RV and wheelchair accessible spaces) near sign indicating Pebble Beach Picnic Area.

TOTAL TRAIL LENGTH & SURFACE:
0.4 mile; hardpacked dirt, gravel.

ALERT:
One incline of 10° occurring 500' into trail.

AMENITIES & FEES:

Vault toilet near parking area, flush toilets and water at Trail Center/Lakeview Picnic Shelter (open year-round), BBQ pits. See pg. 166 for more info on picnic area. Annual or day use state park permit is required and is available at the park office.

NARRATIVE:

Trailhead begins at far corner of parking area on asphalt path near vault toilet. Asphalt will curve to the left after 100' (pg. 66 for details on other trail). Continue straight onto wide, hardpacked dirt/gravel trail. Shortly, you will find two benches to the left and a spectacular photo op of Split Rock Lighthouse. As you descend, views of the Lighthouse and Piney Island become more impressive. Piney Island is a bird sanctuary and closed to foot traffic most of the year.

Before the trail rounds the bend to the right, take time to read the historical marker telling about Little Two Harbors fishing village.

The trail continues into the campground; however, we recommend you turn around here and retrace path to trailhead.

BAYSIDE PARK

Silver Bay, MN • On Highway 61, 52 miles from Duluth

- **A short trek to a scenic overlook delivers great views of Lake Superior, Pellet Island, Marina and hills of Silver Bay.**

DIRECTIONS:

Highway 61 at mile marker 52.4 (watch for sign indicating Marina/Park preceding marker), turn right onto Bayside Park Road to enter park. Take the next right and drive beyond boat launch to upper paved parking lot with ample pull-throughs for trailers and RVs.

TOTAL TRAIL LENGTH & SURFACE:

Approximately 350'; gravel and hardpacked dirt.

ALERT:

Two inclines of 12° each for 15' and 20'.

AMENITIES & FEES:

Portable toilet (seasonal) near picnic area. No fees for trail use.

NARRATIVE:

Trailhead begins in upper parking area at sign indicating overlook. Large platform (guardrails) at trail's end makes a nice viewing area for the above highlights. We think it's worth the trek up!

Father Baraga's Cross (see pg. 139). Photo by Ladona Tornabene

FATHER BARAGA'S CROSS

Cross River
On Highway 61, 79 miles from Duluth

- **A lovely memorial to one of the early Christian missionaries along the North Shore.**
- **Beautiful photo op of the stunning granite cross with Lake Superior as a backdrop.**
- **Dynamic view of Cross River rushing into Lake Superior.**

DIRECTIONS:
Highway 61 at mile marker 79.3, turn right onto Father Baraga Road and follow for 0.2 mile to paved parking area. Note: Drive cautiously as you are in a residential area. Parking is limited.

TOTAL TRAIL LENGTH & SURFACE:
Approximately 200'; hardpacked dirt.

ALERT:
Steep cliffs with no guardrail.

AMENITIES & FEES:
Portable toilet (seasonal), boat launch. There is also a small picnic area (pg. 170) near this location. No fees for trail use.

NARRATIVE:
Trailhead begins at the west side of parking area near sign indicating Father Baraga's Cross. A very short walk reveals a lovely memorial to Father Baraga, missionary to the Native Americans of Madeline Island. The year was 1846 when a raging storm on Lake Superior almost took Father Baraga's life while he was returning from Madeline Island in a small boat. This granite cross today serves as a reminder of the original cross placed on this land by Father Baraga himself to celebrate his safe journey across Lake Superior.

TEMPERANCE RIVER BRIDGE VIEW

Temperance River State Park • On Highway 61, 80 miles from Duluth

- **Experience dramatic views of lower Temperance River rushing through narrow canyon walls with Lake Superior as a backdrop!**
- **Opposite the lake, an expansive view of the Temperance River is impressive as it curves around a birch-lined bend.**

DIRECTIONS:
Highway 61 at mile marker 80.2, pull into paved parking area on either side of highway and either side of Temperance River. There is a special pullout for RVs and campers on left side prior to river. While the state park does not deem it as

such, we speculate that this Almost Hike would be wheelchair accessible in good weather from lake side parking area before the river.

TOTAL TRAIL LENGTH & SURFACE:
100–200' (depending on location of parked vehicle); hardpacked dirt, gravel.

ALERT:
Use caution when crossing Highway 61 and keep children in hand.

AMENITIES & FEES:
Vault toilets in campground on lakeside of highway. No fees for trail use.

NARRATIVE:
Trailhead begins at pedestrian walkways located on either side of the highway bridge. A very short walk delivers a great view and instant photo ops of highlights on this river!

We encourage you to further explore this area via two short hikes and a picnic site that can be accessed from these parking areas (pg. 96, 98, 171).

BEST-KEPT SECRET OF GRAND MARAIS*
Grand Marais, MN • Off Highway 61, 109 miles from Duluth • *Gentle Hikes name

- **Showcases the jagged ridges of the Sawtooth Mountain range, which are thought to be worn remains of ancient volcanoes beautifully silhouetted against Lake Superior.**
- **Vibrant orange lichen nearly covers the rocks.**
- **Commanding views of Grand Marais lighthouse, the Harbor, Artists' Point and Lake Superior.**

DIRECTIONS:
Highway 61 at mile marker 109.1, turn right into Grand Marais Recreation Area and drive 0.3 mile to picnic area 1 (open shelter on the left). Park in gravel lot near boat launch.

TOTAL TRAIL LENGTH & SURFACE:
Length varies depending on how area is explored. Gravel and some flat, level sections of rock.

ALERT:
Some rock surfaces in this area are uneven.

AMENITIES & FEES:
Portable toilet (seasonal). This is also a picnic area (Grand Marais Recreation Area pg. 172) and a boat launch. No fees for trail use.

NARRATIVE:
Trailhead begins at red stairs (two sets of 6 wood steps, 3.5' wide, double handrails) situated between two municipal buildings. These buildings are located off the gravel parking area, close to Lake Superior. There is one bench at bottom of steps. As you ascend, another bench is located at the top of stairs and

affords endless viewing pleasure. To the right are the jagged ridges of the Sawtooth Mountain range. Lake Superior lies directly in front of you and Grand Marais Lighthouse, harbor and Artists' Point are to the left. The rock in this area has some large, very flat sections that can be immediately accessed from the bench. Spend a little time exploring up here.

DEVIL TRACK WILDFLOWER WALK
Gunflint Trail
Off Highway 61, approximately 109 miles from Duluth

- **Plant lovers rejoice! This is the only sanctuary of local flora on the North Shore.**
- **Flora are labeled and bloom at various times throughout the summer.**

DIRECTIONS:
Note: Trailhead is easy to miss. Highway 61 at mile marker 109.4 in Grand Marais, turn left onto the Gunflint Trail (County Road 12) and follow for 5 miles. As you pass County Road 60, the trailhead is located on the right side of the road in precisely 200' marked by a small brown sign indicating Wildflower Sanctuary, 30' prior to guardrail for Devil Track River. Limited parking available on wide gravel/dirt shoulder. (If you pass the lumber mill, turn around and know that you weren't the only one who did so!)

TOTAL TRAIL LENGTH & SURFACE:
0.2 mile (Note: Distances reported in other publications may vary); hardpacked dirt.

ALERT:
Trailhead may be difficult to find. Trail is narrow, averaging 12" wide.

AMENITIES & FEES:
No amenities. No fees for trail use.

NARRATIVE:
Trailhead begins at a small brown sign indicating Wildflower Sanctuary. This is a self- guided trail that is best explored leisurely. You'll want to take your time and savor this educational experience as each plant is labeled and representative of local flora. The trail leads in several directions, but borders Devil Track River to the north, the Gunflint Trail to the west and County Road 60 to the south. We found that the well pump and rough hewn benches formed an irresistibly quaint setting for relaxing along the river and a nice photo op. Enjoy your stroll!

ARTISTS' POINT

Grand Marais, MN • Off Highway 61, 109 miles from Duluth

- **This hike is actually on a peninsula, sporting a variety of luscious flora in a wooded setting.**
- **The rugged shoreline of rock jetties is covered with spectacular, vivid orange lichen.**
- **See the place that has been inspirational to so many artists and you'll definitely know how it acquired its name.**

DIRECTIONS:
Highway 61 at mile marker 109.8, turn right onto Broadway Avenue and follow 0.3 mile to public water access. There is paved parking with wheelchair accessible and RV spaces.

TOTAL TRAIL LENGTH & SURFACE:
0.4 miles (depending on how explored); rock, root and hardpacked dirt, grass.

ALERT:
Gravel driveway en route to Artists' Point is shared with vehicles. Natural rock may be challenging to negotiate in places.

AMENITIES & FEES:
Portable toilets (seasonal), several picnic tables (one with extension), benches, boat launch. No fees for trail use.

NARRATIVE:
Trailhead is located near Coast Guard station at rear of parking lot, to the left of paved/gravel driveway at sign indicating Artists' Point. (Alert: This portion shared with vehicles).

Begin by taking some time to read what's written on the trailhead sign. It's worth the pause. Shortly you will ascend three steps (stone, no handrail) then immediately turn left onto cement sea wall. This leads to some uneven rock negotiation and eventually to a solid rock surface that is basically flat with incredible views of Lake Superior! The 0.4 miles of trails are not definitively marked, but suitable for exploration. Rock and root necessitates careful exploration. This trail is relatively flat and the few inclines/declines that are present can be avoided depending on how the area is explored. Scenery and photo ops abound!

WAYSIDES AND SCENIC LOCALES

We have included the most scenic waysides and overlooks that the North Shore has to offer. Includes stuff you don't even need to leave the car to see!

We tell you which are paved and which have designated wheelchair accessible and RV parking, plus highlights, amenities and a brief narrative of what to expect while there.

Keep in mind that many waysides are closed during snow season. Some only operate seasonally (mid-May to mid-October). This being Minnesota, these are close approximations based on ground freezing and thawing.

Don't forget the camera!

Lower Cascade Falls (see pg. 110). Photo by Melanie Morgan

NORTH SHORE VISITOR CENTER
Duluth, MN

- **Stop at this quaint visitor center for information about Duluth and the North Shore.**
- **Interactive computer kiosk located outside of center.**
- **Grand views of Lake Superior.**

DIRECTIONS:
From Interstate 35 North, continue to end. Follow sign for North Shore, veering right onto London Road. Follow London Road until it ends (name will have changed to Congdon Boulevard). Wayside is at mile marker 5, located to the right directly after crossing the Lester River bridge.

PARKING INFORMATION:
Paved.

AMENITIES:
Visitor center (no water or restrooms).

NARRATIVE:
A charming gazebo is less than 0.1 mile further from Visitor Center and is perfect for family photos. Great place to preserve a memory.

SCENIC HIGHWAY 61
The 19 mile stretch from Duluth to Two Harbors

We're going to break format here because this one merits it. This is not about one wayside, but several and a whole lot more along the way!

EXPLORE
Numerous waysides (many with picnic tables) sprawled in intervals throughout this two lane, 19 mile stretch of highway—all with breathtaking Lake Superior views.

BICYCLE
The highway's shoulder (paved, but can have gravel) is a designated bike path. And the views of Superior are stupendous!

RUN
Each year in June, Scenic Highway 61 is the location of Grandma's Marathon. This annual race is a world-class event drawing competitors from many nations. It begins near Two Harbors and continues along the shoreline drive into Duluth, with its completion in Canal Park.

FISH
The French River is a hatchery for Rainbow and Chinook trout. The French and Knife Rivers are also designated trout streams.

EAT

A few restaurants have located along this wonderfully scenic stretch of highway. Two of our favorites are the New Scenic Café (excellent pistachio encrusted goat cheese salad) and Emily's (outstanding fish chowder!). Both are smoke-free.

SHOP

Quaint gift and specialty shops are located in various places along Highway 61, with some offering items unique to this geographical region.

STAY

From campgrounds to cabins to motel/hotel-style lodging, you'll find it here. But get your reservations in early! Accommodations can be found all the way up the North Shore to the Canadian Border.

SKI

The entire North Shore is nirvana for cross-country skiers!

FRENCH RIVER HATCHERY

On Scenic Highway 61, 6 miles from highway entrance in Duluth

- **Fisherman's Paradise! Hatchery for Rainbow and Chinook trout.**
- **Designated trout stream.**
- **Tour the DNR Fish Hatchery (seasonal).**

DIRECTIONS:

Scenic Highway 61 at French River wayside (located immediately after crossing French River), turn right into parking area. If you wish to tour the DNR Fish Hatchery, take the second driveway to the left after crossing river.

PARKING INFORMATION:

Paved; designated wheelchair accessible parking.

AMENITIES:

Portable toilet (seasonal).

NARRATIVE:

This is definitely a hot fishing spot, and heavily used. A paved trail (approximately 300') leads under Highway 61 bridge along this designated trout stream shaded by cedars. Trout fishing is allowed above Highway 61 expressway, but not from that location to the mouth of French River. Trout eggs are collected each spring during spawning season. This is also the location of Natural Resources Department of Fisheries, which offers free, self-guided tours.

BUCHANAN HISTORICAL MARKER

On Scenic Highway 61, 11 miles from highway entrance in Duluth

- **This old wayside was built to commemorate the town of Buchanan, named for our 15th President, James Buchanan.**
- **Buchanan was the seat of the land office for the northeastern district of Minnesota.**
- **Beautiful vista of Lake Superior.**

DIRECTIONS:
On Scenic Highway 61, opposite fire number 5875. Parking on pull-off.

PARKING INFORMATION:
Paved

AMENITIES:
None

NARRATIVE:
Descend either set of 12 steps (stone, no handrail) from the road level to the viewing area of this quaint wayside and historical marker. A few feet beyond that is Lake Superior's shore.

KNIFE RIVER WAYSIDE

Highway 61 Expressway, 18 miles from Duluth

- **The memorial here was dedicated in recognition of Arthur V. Rohweder in 1961 for his work and success in accident prevention.**
- **This wayside overlooks the lovely Knife River.**

DIRECTIONS:
Highway 61 Expressway at mile marker 18.8 (watch for sign indicating wayside rest preceding marker), turn right and follow signs.

PARKING INFORMATION:
Paved; designated wheelchair accessible and RV parking.

AMENITIES:
Vault toilets, picnic tables (two open-sided shelters; two of the tables under the shelters have extensions), pavement extends to all tables.

NARRATIVE:
A very nice, well-manicured wayside. Knife River is a designated trout stream and two sets of steps–40 then 17 (all wood, double handrail, non-continuous)–take you to river's edge.

LIGHTHOUSE POINT PUBLIC WATER ACCESS*

Off Highway 61, 26 miles from Duluth • *Gentle Hikes name

- **This is a great picnic area with delightful views of Lake Superior and Agate Bay. You can observe active ore docks in fairly close proximity while watching boats the size of three football fields!**

- **See the original Two Harbors Lighthouse, which began operation in 1892 and continues today making it the oldest operating lighthouse in Minnesota.**

- **See the fishing boat** *Crusader II* **that was built in 1939 and christened by Norway's Crown Prince Olav.**

DIRECTIONS:

Highway 61 at mile marker 26 (Note: You will not find actual mile marker— use odometer reading from marker 25), turn right onto Waterfront Drive (corner of Dairy Queen and Blackwoods Restaurant) and follow for 0.5 mile to South Avenue. Turn left and follow for 0.3 mile to 3rd Street; turn right and follow for 0.2 mile to parking area.

PARKING INFORMATION:

Paved; ample RV parking.

AMENITIES:

Portable toilets (seasonal), picnic tables, boat launch, small gift shop in lighthouse.

NARRATIVE:

Several picnic tables and benches are scattered around the perimeter of the parking area. All have great views of Lake Superior and the harbor between the lighthouse and the ore docks. This is also the parking area for the Sonju Harbor Walking Trail (Lighthouse Loop) hike and Breakwater Lighthouse Point Stroll, an Almost Hike, (pg. 52, 135).

 Foot Note:

Tours of the lighthouse are available May through October (1-888-832-5606).

FLOOD BAY WAYSIDE

On Highway 61, 27 miles from Duluth

- **Incredible views of Lake Superior—especially striking when waves are crashing on the shore!**
- **Direct access to water's edge with ample opportunity to search for agates along the pebble beach.**

DIRECTIONS:

Highway 61 at mile marker 27.5 (watch for sign preceding marker), turn right into Flood Bay Wayside parking area.

PARKING INFORMATION:

Paved; designated wheelchair accessible and RV parking. Day use area only.

AMENITIES:

Vault toilet—wheelchair accessible.

NARRATIVE:

We think this is one of the best waysides for viewing wave action! It brings you very close to Lake Superior. Four sets of stone steps (no handrails) take you to a wide pebble beach just around the bay from Superior Shores Resort. With every storm, the lake washes stones up on the beach. Join the hunt for agates at the water's edge or just kick back and enjoy the sights and sounds of Superior.

Split Rock Lighthouse (see pg. 68). Photo by Ladona Tornabene

STEWART RIVER WAYSIDE*

On Highway 61, 33 miles from Duluth • *Gentle Hikes name

- **Up-close view highlighting some of Superior's famous rugged shoreline.**
- **Views of the lovely Stewart River.**

DIRECTIONS:
Highway 61 at mile marker 33.7, after crossing bridge, turn right into gravel lot across from Betty's Pies.

PARKING INFORMATION:
Gravel.

AMENITIES:
Portable toilets (seasonal). Cart and carry official public water access located near bridge (descend 25 steps, cement, no rail).

NARRATIVE:
We found this quaint little wayside a fun place to experiment with photography because it offers views of the Stewart River framed under the bridge, plus Superior's rugged coastline—especially photogenic when waves are crashing! However, if it's your taste buds that want to record a memory… Betty's Pies, located right across the highway, is open year-round serving breakfast, lunch and dinner in a smoke-free environment.

 Foot Note:

Betty's Pies offers over 50 varieties of pie. Some are made from original 1950s recipes developed by Betty herself; some are sugar-free. (218-834-3367 or www.bettyspies.com)

SPLIT ROCK WAYSIDE

On Highway 61, 45 miles from Duluth

- **Grand view of Split Rock Lighthouse—right from your car!**
- **A marker here provides information about the geology of the Split Rock and Beaver Bay area.**

DIRECTIONS:
Highway 61 at mile marker 45.2 (watch for sign indicating wayside preceding marker), veer right into pullout.

PARKING INFORMATION:
Paved; highway pull-through.

AMENITIES:
A couple of weathered picnic tables.

NARRATIVE:

Excellent and popular photo op. On a clear day, this is a lovely area from which to view the lighthouse.

 Foot Note:

The paved Gitchi Gami Trail, originating in Two Harbors and continuing to Grand Marais, was under construction at time of writing, but eventually will run through the wooded area of this wayside.

PALISADE HEAD OVERLOOK
On Highway 61, 57 miles from Duluth

- **A glorious view of Shovel Point to the left and the Sawtooth Range to the right. On a clear day, look for the Apostle Islands in the distance.**
- **Rills of igneous rhyolite overlaying softer basalt combine to form Palisade and Shovel Point.**
- **Before driving up, stop at the initial pullout and read the marker regarding formation of the North Shore as we know it today.**

DIRECTIONS:

Highway 61 at mile marker 57, turn right and travel 0.4 mile to the top on a paved, curvy road through a splendid mixed forest. Alert: Sharp curves, no trailers or RVs allowed. Two-way road is very narrow and steep in places.

PARKING INFORMATION:

Paved.

AMENITIES:

None.

NARRATIVE:

Definitely joy in the journey here! Not only are the views striking from the top, but the short drive up is spectacular in and of itself as you wind your way up the narrow road through a splendid mixed forest. Seems like entering another world just yards off the highway. Palisade is a favorite of rock climbers.

ALERT:

When at the top, use extreme caution when walking over to view Palisade Head. There is no trail and rock surfaces require careful negotiation. The viewing cliff is very steep and there are no guardrails, only a brick barrier.

CROSS RIVER WAYSIDE

On Highway 61, 79 miles from Duluth

- **Dramatic cascades of the Cross River can be seen from highway, but we highly recommend a stop and a camera!**
- **Overlooks on both sides of bridge from pedestrian walkway.**
- **A memorial to Father Frederic Baraga, pioneer missionary to the early residents along the North Shore, is here.**

DIRECTIONS:
Highway 61 at mile marker 78.9, pull into parking area on left side of highway prior to bridge.

PARKING INFORMATION:
Paved; designated wheelchair accessible, motorcycle and RV parking.

AMENITIES:
Vault toilets (wheelchair accessible); polished granite benches.

NARRATIVE:
We highly recommend parking in one of the designated areas as there is no stopping allowed on highway to view these roaring cascades.

The cascades are very visible from the 6–8' wide cement sidewalk on the bridge (wheelchair accessible). Alert: Use caution when crossing Highway 61 and keep children in hand.

In addition to the stunning cascades, a new overlook (guardrail) has been added on lake side of highway, providing a view of the Cross River's lower gorge. A trek down 37 newly built steps (wood, handrail, non-continuous) offers a closer look.

CASCADE RIVER WAYSIDE

On Highway 61, 100 miles from Duluth • *Gentle Hikes name

- **Gorgeous view of Lake Superior!**
- **A short trek down a few steps showcases the Cascade River as it flows into Lake Superior.**

DIRECTIONS:
Highway 61 at mile marker 99.9, veer right into pullout.

PARKING INFORMATION:
Paved; highway pull-through.

AMENITIES:
None.

This one is often crowded and with good reason. Breathtaking lake views combined with its proximity to Cascade River State Park and Lower Cascade Falls Quick Route (pg. 106) make it an ideal stopping place.

To get a view of the Cascade as it flows into Superior, descend the 25 steps (stone and wood, some handrail, non-continuous) located at the northeast side of parking area.

GOOD HARBOR BAY WAYSIDE
On Highway 61, 104 miles from Duluth

- **See and read about what happened when lava flows explosively encountered standing water.**
- **Beautiful view of Good Harbor Bay and rugged shoreline of Lake Superior.**

DIRECTIONS:
Highway 61 at mile marker 104.1 (watch for historical marker sign preceding mile marker), veer right into pullout.

PARKING INFORMATION:
Paved; highway pull-through.

AMENITIES:
None.

NARRATIVE:
A must-see for those with an unquenchable geological hunger! Explanations of the geology of the area and historical significance are displayed on informational plates. Wheelchair accessible.

CUTFACE CREEK REST AREA
On Highway 61, 104 miles from Duluth

- **Sit among old growth pine and stately birch.**
- **Manicured lawns sport very nice picnic tables overlooking the lake; paved walkways lead to strategically placed benches for Superior views!**
- **Walking access to water's edge.**

DIRECTIONS:
Highway 61 at mile marker 104.5, turn right into Cutface Creek rest area.

PARKING INFORMATION:
Paved; designated wheelchair accessible and RV parking.

AMENITIES:

Vault toilets (wheelchair accessible), picnic tables (paved path extends to one table), benches.

NARRATIVE:

We think this wayside has something for nearly everyone. It brings you to water's edge via a paved path leading to 11 wide steps (rock, no handrail), then onto a pebble beach. Strategically placed benches afford viewing pleasure from any angle. To date, we say it's one of the best-groomed waysides on the shore.

PINCUSHION MOUNTAIN OVERLOOK

Off Highway 61, approximately 109 miles from Duluth

- **The only designated drive-to overlook that features an aerial view of Grand Marais Harbor, Lighthouse and Artists' Point with nearly panoramic views of Lake Superior.**
- **Showcases the jagged ridges of the Sawtooth Mountain range, which are thought to be worn remains of ancient volcanoes beautifully silhouetted against Lake Superior.**

DIRECTIONS:

Highway 61 at mile marker 109.4, turn left onto the Gunflint Trail (County Road 12) and follow for 2 miles. Turn right onto Pincushion Drive (County Road 53) and follow for 0.1 mile to overlook.

PARKING INFORMATION:

Paved (Fall 2001); no designated spaces at that time. Parking area is loop- shaped, which may accommodate RV pull-through.

AMENITIES:

Vault toilet (wheelchair accessible).

NARRATIVE:

Delightful views of the above highlights generously framed by evergreens. When viewing the harbor, Eagle Mountain will be to the right and the Sawtooth Mountain range located beyond it. Informational board provided is wheelchair accessible.

GRAND MARAIS PUBLIC WATER ACCESS

(a.k.a. Boulder Park)

Off Highway 61, approximately 109 miles from Duluth

- **A drive-to view of Grand Marais Harbor, Artist Point, Lighthouse, Eagle Mountain, Pincushion Mountain, Sawtooth Mountain range.**
- **Picnic tables with great lake and harbor views.**
- **Former site of pulp wood rafting.**

DIRECTIONS:
Highway 61 at mile marker 109.8, turn right onto Broadway Avenue and follow 0.3 mile to public water access.

PARKING INFORMATION:
Paved; designated wheelchair accessible and RV parking.

AMENITIES:
Portable toilets (seasonal), several picnic tables (one with extension), benches, boat launch.

NARRATIVE:
This popular area is conveniently located in the heart of Grand Marais with several restaurants and specialty shops nearby. This is also the parking area for the Artists' Point Almost Hike and the Lighthouse Stroll (pg. 142, 116). The scenery is rich—right from the car! Views of Pincushion Mountain to the north, Eagle Mountain to the west and the Sawtooth Mountain range located thirty miles to the southwest. Not to mention what's in our highlights above. Enjoy!

 Foot Note:

There's much to see and do in Grand Marais. Contact the Visitor Information Center (800-622-4014 or www.grandmaraismn.com)

Good Harbor Bay Wayside (see pg. 155). Photo by Ladona Tornabene

KADUNCE RIVER WAYSIDE

On Highway 61, 119 miles from Duluth

- **The town of Colvill was named in honor of Colonel William Colvill, Commander of 1st Minnesota Regiment, which was present at many major battles during the Civil War.**
- **Great place for a sunrise or sunset picnic.**
- **Listen for the comforting sounds of waves on the pebble beach.**

DIRECTIONS:
Highway 61 at mile marker 118.9, after crossing bridge, turn right into Kadunce River Wayside paved parking lot (highway sign is spelled Kodonce).

PARKING INFORMATION:
Paved; designated wheelchair accessible and motorcycle parking.

AMENITIES:
Picnic table with pavement extending to it.

NARRATIVE:
A small, lovely wayside showcasing Lake Superior with access to water's edge via a pebble beach. Kadunce Creek empties into the lake here.

OLD DOG TRAIL*

Off Highway 61, 128 miles from Duluth • *Gentle Hikes name

- **This is part of the historic John Beargrease sled-dog route. When road-ways were impassible due to snow, mail and supplies were shipped to this location, then packed on a dog sled for delivery.**
- **Great view of Superior's rugged shoreline.**

DIRECTIONS:
Highway 61 at mile marker 128.4 (as you enter Hovland), turn right onto Chicago Bay Street and follow for 0.1 mile to old pier and boat launch.

PARKING INFORMATION:
Paved. Not what you'd typically expect—very minimal parking and what we saw was not well maintained—but we included it because of its historical significance.

AMENITIES:
Boat launch

NARRATIVE:
This wayside literally brings you within feet of the waters of Superior; however, do not drive on pier due to instability issues. Old Dog Trail, which ran along the North Shore for 130 miles, was used for mail delivery between Grand Marais and Fort William, Canada. This wayside is the original mail drop location.

GRAND PORTAGE BAY REST AREA
On Highway 61, 146 miles from Duluth

- **Visitor center packed with brochures. Also houses information regarding determination of U.S. and Canadian border.**
- **Gorgeous view of Lake Superior off back deck and splendid wooded picnic areas (some fairly secluded).**

DIRECTIONS:
Highway 61 at mile marker 146, turn left at sign indicating rest area and follow for 0.2 mile.

PARKING INFORMATION:
Paved, designated wheelchair accessible and RV parking.

AMENITIES:
Flush toilets, water (both seasonal). In addition to wooded picnic settings, there are three tables located on paved entrance level; one is covered.

NARRATIVE:
This one's worth the stop. Have a picnic here. Notice the intriguing rock formations. Read a little about history and pick up some informational brochures. This is the best-stocked rest stop beyond Grand Marais. Have fun.

ISLE ROYALE AND SUSIE ISLANDS
Overlook #1*
On Highway 61, 147 miles from Duluth • *Gentle Hikes name

- **A sweeping panorama of the Susie Islands in the foreground and (on a clear day) Isle Royale beyond.**
- **Picturesque photo ops.**

DIRECTIONS:
Highway 61 at mile marker 147.5 (watch for sign indicating Scenic Overlook preceding marker), turn right into parking area. Actual wayside is partially hidden from highway.

PARKING INFORMATION:
Paved; designated RV parking.

AMENITIES:
One lone weathered picnic table, vault toilets (wheelchair accessible).

NARRATIVE:
A nice 'away from the highway' parking area offering some lovely scenery on a clear day. Views abound from the car, but it's a great stretch break!

ISLE ROYALE AND SUSIE ISLANDS

Overlook #2*

On Highway 61, 148 miles from Duluth • *Gentle Hikes name

- **This one is very similar to overlook #1, but offers a closer look at the Susie Islands in the foreground and (on a clear day) Isle Royale beyond.**

DIRECTIONS:

Highway 61 at mile marker 148.1, veer right into pullout. This wayside is directly on Highway 61.

PARKING INFORMATION:

Paved; highway pull-through.

AMENITIES:

None.

NARRATIVE:

In a hurry or just don't feel like getting the entire family out of the vehicle again? Look no further, because this one has great views right from the car! If it's clear out, this one's worth the brief pull-off so the driver can enjoy it, too.

High Falls at Grand Portage (see pg. 128). Photo by Ladona Tornabene

PICNIC AREAS

Whether you grill it or pack it, we have selected some of the most scenic picnic areas along Lake Superior and the North Shore. From woods to rivers and the big lake, you'll find all kinds of picnic spots listed here. Bon appetit!

We had a little fun writing the picnic areas in a "Menu" format featuring 'Appetizers,' 'Main Course,' and 'Dessert.'

APPETIZER:

Typically we list what is nearby and en route to the picnic area (what precedes it—as an appetizer precedes a meal), be it an Almost Hike, trail or wayside.

MAIN COURSE:

Here's where we describe what the actual picnic area is like.

DESSERT:

Usually we list what is nearby the picnic area—be it an Almost Hike, trail or area to explore. It's what we recommend as a great finish to a good meal, but actually burns calories instead!

In addition, we include amenities (located at the picnic area sites), applicable fees, parking surface and designated wheelchair accessible spaces. We also note sites that have pavement extending to tables and/or table extensions.

Please note: All tables are park and carry, unless otherwise noted.

Beach at Temperance River Picnic Area (see pg. 171). Photo by Ladona Tornabene

KITCHI GAMMI PARK
(a.k.a. Brighton Beach)
Duluth, MN

- **Appetizer: En route to this picnic area, stop for a family photo op. There is a gazebo just prior to the entrance of Brighton Beach that affords glorious views of Lake Superior and a resting place for the travel-weary. Great place to preserve a memory.**

- **Main Course: This scenic 0.8 mile stretch of road hugs Lake Superior and offers numerous places to picnic among gorgeous lake and wooded sites. There is also a playground and a place to build a fire. A true luxury—right here in Duluth.**

- **Dessert: Explore! Explore! Explore!**

PICNIC AREA DIRECTIONS:
From Interstate 35 North, continue to end. Follow sign for North Shore, veering right onto London Road. Follow London Road until it ends (name will have changed to Congdon Boulevard). At mile marker 5.1, veer right onto paved road for Brighton Beach entrance.

PARKING INFORMATION:
Gravel and paved areas available. Some tables can be driven to; all others are park and carry. Tables are moveable.

AMENITIES & FEES:
Portable toilets (seasonal), playground, fire bunker, open-sided shelter, grills, BBQ pits. No fees for picnic area use.

LAKEVIEW PARK PICNIC AREA
Burlington Bay Area • Off Highway 61, 26 miles from Duluth

- **Appetizer: En route to picnic area, stop at Burlington Bay for some serious stone skipping. So prime is the spot that it's home to an annual contest!**

- **Main Course: It feels out in the woods, yet you're in the middle of town when dining here. A covered shelter offers partial lake and wooded views.**

- **Dessert: Take a leisurely stroll on the nearby Sonju Harbor Walking Trail (from Burlington Bay to First Street pg. 54). It's a lovely paved path with many benches and gratifying lake views.**

PICNIC AREA DIRECTIONS:
Highway 61 at mile marker 26.4 (Note: you will not find actual mile marker—use odometer reading from marker 25; after passing through the main area of Two Harbors, watch for sign indicating Burlington Bay Campground), turn right onto First Street and follow for 0.3 mile. Look for picnic area on the right. Parking available on roadside along First Street.

PARKING INFORMATION:
Paved along roadside.

AMENITIES & FEES:
Grills, flush toilets (seasonal) at covered shelter, playground equipment.
No fees for picnic area use.

Upper Gooseberry Falls (see pg. 56). Photo by Ladona Tornabene

GOOSEBERRY FALLS PICNIC AREAS

Gooseberry Falls State Park • On Highway 61, 39 miles from Duluth

- **Appetizer: Take the 5 minute stroll on a paved path to see spectacular Gooseberry Falls (pg. 56), the most visited area on the North Shore!**

- **Main Course: Historical Lakeview Shelter (fully enclosed), is equipped with fireplace and lots of windows. Nearby are a variety of tables, some wooded, others with commanding lake views. Feeling nostalgic? Check out the vintage tables near the mouth of the river.**

- **Dessert: A short spur near the Lakeview Shelter parking area takes you to the mouth of Gooseberry River. The pebble beach area is ideal for watching waves crash on rocky outcrops!**

PICNIC AREA DIRECTIONS:
Highway 61 at mile marker 38.9, turn right into Gooseberry Falls State Park and follow signs to picnic area that is located approximately 1 mile from the Visitor Center.

PARKING INFORMATION:
Small paved parking is located in front of Lakeview Picnic shelter; larger paved parking is less than 0.1 mile further at picnic area.

AMENITIES & FEES:
Flush toilets and water (both seasonal) at Lakeview Shelter, vault toilet, BBQ pits and grills. Annual or day use state park permit is required and is available at the Visitor Center. Lakeview Shelter rental fees. Contact park office: (218) 834-3855.

 Foot Note:

Lakeview Shelter was constructed in 1934 by the Civilian Conservation Corps (CCC) and is part of 624 acres at the park listed on the Historic Registry.

PEBBLE BEACH PICNIC AREA

Split Rock Lighthouse State Park • On Highway 61, 46 miles from Duluth

- **Appetizer: Take a stroll on the paved portion of the Little Two Harbors Trail (pg. 68) to select the best picnic site. A variety of lake and wooded sites available.**

- **Main Course: Beautiful birch forest with captivating views of Lake Superior and Piney Island!**

- **Dessert: Try the Almost Hike to Pebble Beach (pg. 136) for awe-inspiring views of Split Rock Lighthouse and Piney Island.**

PICNIC AREA DIRECTIONS:
Highway 61 at mile marker 45.9, turn right into Split Rock Lighthouse State

Park. Follow past Visitor Center turning right onto the first street you encounter. Follow for 0.5 mile to parking lot near sign indicating Pebble Beach Picnic Area.

PARKING INFORMATION:
Paved; designated wheelchair accessible and RV parking.

AMENITIES & FEES:
Vault toilet (wheelchair accessible) near parking area, flush toilets and water at Trail Center/Lakeview Picnic Shelter (open year-round), BBQ pits. Annual or day use state park permit is required and is available at the park office.

TRAIL CENTER/LAKEVIEW PICNIC AREA
Split Rock Lighthouse State Park • On Highway 61, 46 miles from Duluth

- **Appetizer: Take a spur off the Little Two Harbors trail located directly outside the shelter for unsurpassed views of Split Rock Lighthouse. Definitely bring the camera.**

- **Main Course: Near a birch forest are two shelters that offer a unique dining experience. Wood burning stove, beautifully finished picnic tables, reading materials about the North Shore and photos of Split Rock Lighthouse State Park highlights are all located in the fully enclosed side of the shelter. The partially enclosed side of the shelter provides enough tables and two grills to accommodate even the biggest of families.**

- **Dessert: Take the entire Little Two Harbors Trail (pg. 68). If you're a birch lover, this is paradise!**

PICNIC AREA DIRECTIONS:
Highway 61 at mile marker 45.9, turn right into Split Rock Lighthouse State Park. Follow past visitor center turning right onto the first street you encounter. Follow for 0.4 mile and turn left at sign indicating Trail Center and Lakeview Picnic Area.

PARKING INFORMATION:
Paved; designated wheelchair accessible and RV parking.

AMENITIES & FEES:
Flush toilets and water fountain open year-round. Both shelters are wheelchair accessible. Annual or day use state park permit is required and is available at the park office. For shelter reservations, call the park office: (218) 226-6372.

Note: The open-sided shelter at opposite end of parking area is paved and has a paved trail with a decline of 10° (18% grade) for 30', which becomes the incline upon return.

BAYSIDE PARK PICNIC AREA

Silver Bay Marina & Park • On Highway 61, 52 miles from Duluth

- **Appetizer: Take the paved walk out toward the flag circle. If fog is lingering on the lake, you may experience an especially striking view of Pellet Island.**
- **Main Course: Picnic areas are generously scattered around the park offering a variety of Lake Superior and wooded views. Boat launch available.**
- **Dessert: Take the Bayside Park Almost Hike (pg. 137) up to a scenic overlook with first-rate views of the safe harbor and lake.**

PICNIC AREA DIRECTIONS:

Highway 61 at mile marker 52.4 (watch for sign indicating Marina/Park preceding marker), turn right onto Bayside Park Road to enter park.

PARKING INFORMATION:

Parking (paved and gravel) is plentiful and scattered throughout the marina; however, no trailers allowed in picnic areas. A generous gravel lot for RVs and trailers is available by taking the first left upon entering the park.

Designated parking for wheelchair accessibility; however, the spaces are gravel with very close proximity to picnic tables (with extensions) at open-sided shelters.

AMENITIES & FEES:

Vault toilets, BBQ pits, grills, playground. Silver Bay Safe Harbor and boat launch. No fees for picnic area use.

TETTEGOUCHE GENERAL PICNIC AREAS*

Tettegouche State Park • On Highway 61, 58 miles from Duluth • *Gentle Hikes name

- **Appetizer: Hike the gorgeous Shovel Point Trail (pg. 76).**
- **Main Course: Your choice of some fine wooded settings or lake views.**
- **Dessert: Take the 0.4 mile Baptism River Loop trail (pg. 80) nearby.**

PICNIC AREA DIRECTIONS:

Highway 61 at mile marker 58.5, turn right into Tettegouche State Park and follow to paved parking area straight ahead. There is also a paved parking lot for RVs near the recycle bins. Picnic areas can be accessed from the parking lot. A large wooded section is located directly across the road from the Visitor Center. Several tables are also scattered about the paved trail leading to Shovel Point trailhead (pg. 76).

PARKING INFORMATION:

Paved; designated wheelchair accessible parking and separate lot for RVs.

AMENITIES & FEES:

Visitor Center with gift shop, informational displays, flush toilets and water fountain. On paved trail, pavement extends to tables. Annual or day use state park permit is required and is available at the park office.

HIGH FALLS PICNIC AREA

Tettegouche State Park • On Highway 61, 58 miles from Duluth

- **Appetizer: Trek to High Falls of Tettegouche (pg. 84). Worth the trip!**
- **Main Course: Dine in a beautiful wooded environment preserved with careful attention to privacy.**
- **Dessert: Listen for bird calls.**

PICNIC AREA DIRECTIONS:

Highway 61 at mile marker 58.5, turn right into Tettegouche State Park and immediately take another right passing Visitor Center (picnic area is located 1.5 miles beyond Visitor Center). Drive downhill, cross bridge and follow signs to Trail Center where parking and sign indicating picnic area are located.

PARKING INFORMATION:

Paved; designated RV parking.

AMENITIES & FEES:

Vault toilet, BBQ pits. Annual or day use state park permit is required and is available at the park office.

BENSEN LAKE PICNIC AREA

George H. Crosby-Manitou State Park • Off Highway 61, approximately 59 miles from Duluth

- **Appetizer: Relax on the strategically placed bench that affords a full view of Bensen Lake. Watch for otters and loons.**

- **Main Course: This beautiful gem of a lake has shaded and sunny lakeside picnic sites.**

- **Dessert: Hike the vibrant moss-covered forest floors of Bensen Lake Trail (pg. 88).**

PICNIC AREA DIRECTIONS:

Highway 61 at mile marker 59.3, turn left onto County Road 1 and follow for 6.2 miles (you will travel through Finland). Turn right onto County Road 7 and follow for 7.6 miles. Turn right onto Bensen Lake Road (also Fire #7616) into George H. Crosby-Manitou State Park and follow for 0.5 mile to gravel parking lot on left.

PARKING INFORMATION:

Picnic area is 0.1 mile from gravel parking lot (follow sign for Bensen Lake Trail); however, there is a spot where you can park temporarily to unload picnic supplies.

AMENITIES & FEES:

Vault toilet (wheelchair accessible), water available (seasonal) at park entrance, BBQ pit. Annual or day use state park permit is required. A pay box is available at the park entrance.

 Foot Note:

This is the most remote of all North Shore state parks and is managed by Tettegouche State Park.

FATHER BARAGA'S CROSS PICNIC AREA*

Shroeder, MN • On Highway 61, 79 miles from Duluth • *Gentle Hikes name

- **Appetizer: The cascades of Cross River Wayside (pg. 154) merit a stop; just prior to the turn-off for this picnic area.**
- **Main Course: Gorgeous lake site, but there are only a couple of tables here.**
- **Dessert: We encourage you to stroll down to Father Baraga's Cross (pg. 139), a tribute to the original cross erected by Father Baraga himself in 1846 to commemorate a safe crossing during a violent Lake Superior storm while returning from a missionary trip.**

PICNIC AREA DIRECTIONS:
Highway 61 at mile marker 79.3, turn right onto Father Baraga Road and follow for 0.2 mile to parking area. Alert: Drive cautiously as you are in a residential area.

PARKING INFORMATION:
Paved; limited parking.

AMENITIES & FEES:
Portable toilet (seasonal), grill, BBQ pit, boat launch. No fees for picnic area use.

TEMPERANCE RIVER PICNIC AREA

Temperance River State Park • On Highway 61, 80 miles from Duluth

- **Appetizer: We recommend the extraordinary Cauldron Trail (pg. 98) nearby, which features seven dramatic overlooks!**
- **Main Course: Fabulous vista of Lake Superior and its pebble beach.**
- **Dessert: Check out the Temperance River Lower Loop (pg. 96).**

PICNIC AREA DIRECTIONS:
Highway 61 at mile marker 80.2 (turn off is easy to miss; watch for fire marker 7680), turn right at picnic area sign prior to Temperance River and follow for 0.1 mile to picnic area.

PARKING INFORMATION:
One spot is paved, the remainder are gravel. In some places, parking can be very close to tables.

AMENITIES & FEES:
Vault toilets (wheelchair accessible), water (seasonal), BBQ pit. Annual or day use state park permit is required to enter park or picnic area and is available at the park office.

CASCADE RIVER STATE PARK PICNIC AREA

Cascade River State Park • On Highway 61, 100 miles from Duluth

- **Appetizer: If you like waterfalls, take the Lower Cascade Falls Quick Route (pg. 106).**
- **Main Course: Picnic in a secluded wooded environment with stunning views of Lake Superior.**
- **Dessert: Hike the Lake Superior Shore Trail (pg. 108), which showcases unlimited views of the greatest of the Great Lakes.**

PICNIC AREA DIRECTIONS:

Highway 61 at mile marker 100.3, veer right into Cascade River State Park Picnic Area (a long pull-through section of road). Although there is no parking lot per se, parking is permitted in this area.

PARKING INFORMATION:

Paved/gravel alongside pull-through section of road. Nearest tables are located approximately 200' from parking area; others are further.

AMENITIES & FEES:

Vault toilet, grills, BBQ pits. Annual or day use state park permit is required to enter park or picnic area and is available at the park office.

GRAND MARAIS RECREATION AREA

Grand Marais, MN • On Highway 61, 109 miles from Duluth

- **Appetizer: Work up an appetite strolling around Grand Marais for the day!**
- **Main Course: Commanding views of Lake Superior, Grand Marais Harbor, Artists' Point and Lighthouse from a covered open-sided shelter.**
- **Dessert: We highly recommend Best-Kept Secret of Grand Marais Almost Hike (pg. 140).**

PICNIC AREA DIRECTIONS:

Highway 61 at mile marker 109.1, turn right into Grand Marais Recreation Area and follow for 0.3 mile to Picnic Area 1 (open-sided shelter on left).

PARKING INFORMATION:

Gravel parking area is less than 10' from paved shelter. Note: There is no ramp access from gravel lot to shelter 1, but tables are moveable.

AMENITIES & FEES:

Portable toilet (seasonal), grill, one table with extensions at both ends. No fees for picnic area use.

GRAND PORTAGE NATIONAL MONUMENT PICNIC AREA

Grand Portage, MN • Off Highway 61, approximately 144 miles from Duluth

- **Appetizer: Excellent opportunity to visit the Grand Portage National Monument.**

- **Main Course: Picnic by Lake Superior nestled beneath the hills of Grand Portage and majestic white spruce.**

- **Dessert: Take a stroll on the spur trails that lead to the lake, monument and through a refreshing stand of pine.**

PICNIC AREA DIRECTIONS:

Highway 61 at mile marker 144.6, turn right onto Stevens Road. At Y in road, veer right and follow sign toward National Monument. At second stop sign, turn left onto Mile Creek Road for picnic area (0.1 mile from monument parking area) or stop at the monument and take a tour first.

PARKING INFORMATION:

Paved at monument with designated wheelchair accessible parking; gravel at picnic area overflow with no designated spaces.

AMENITIES & FEES:

Flush toilets (seasonal, open 8 a.m.–5 p.m.) near monument. Restrooms are wheelchair accessible; however, pathway leading to them was being planned for renovation as of 8/01. Parking at monument and picnic area is free. Fees charged for monument entrance only.

 Foot Note:

The Monument presents an incredible lesson in history through costumed reenactment (open Memorial Day through early October) (218) 387-2788 or www.nps.gov/grpo

GRAND PORTAGE STATE PARK PICNIC AREA

Grand Portage State Park • On Highway 61, 150 miles from Duluth

---

- **Appetizer: Scope out the best sites along this 0.2 mile stroll and while you're at it, meander another 280' to read up on the Webster-Ashburton Treaty of 1842 between the U.S. and Canada, (pg. 126).**

- **Main Course: Wonderfully wooded "off the beaten path" picnic sites with fabulous views of the Pigeon River.**

- **Dessert: One that actually burns calories...Take the 1.0 mile round trip hike on a very level paved trail to spectacular High Falls (pg. 128), highest in the entire state!**

PICNIC AREA DIRECTIONS:

Highway 61 at mile marker 150.6, turn left into Grand Portage State Park (if you miss it, you'll be turning around at customs because you're practically at the border!). Parking is located at park entrance. Picnic area is located across from Visitor Center by sign indicating same.

PARKING INFORMATION:

Paved; designated wheelchair accessible parking. It is approximately 300' from the parking lot to the first picnic site (excluding the lone table that may be available at the park entrance).

AMENITIES & FEES:

Visitor Center, gift shop and vault toilet (all wheelchair accessible). No drinking fountains available. Bring your own water. Annual or day use state park permit is required and is available at the park office.

Note: Although the trail is paved to the picnic area, the actual paths leading to the tables are not.

HIKING FOR HEALTH

INCREDIBLE STUFF EVEN WE COULDN'T MAKE UP!

It's been said that if the beneficial effects of exercise could be put into pill form, it would easily be a trillion dollar seller!

The health benefits of walking/hiking are phenomenal! These benefits extend beyond the obvious physical component of health. They encompass the psychological (mental and emotional), social and spiritual components of health as well.

Let's begin by taking a quick glance at the physical health of our nation. Let's look at the cons of being inactive as well as the pros of being active so that you don't have to become one of the nation's statistics.

Drawbacks of Inactivity and Benefits of Physical Activity

Physical inactivity alone is responsible for over a quarter million deaths in this country every year according to the Centers for Disease Control.[1]

Physical activity will reduce the risk of death due to inactivity.

Heart disease is the number one killer of both men and women in this nation.

Exercise such as walking or hiking can help prevent heart attacks and heart disease for both men and women.[2,3]

It has been known for a long time that inactive people have nearly twice the risk of developing heart disease as active people.[4]

Walking briskly for 5 or more hours per week can reduce the risk of heart attack by 50%. [2]

An estimated 60% of Americans are inactive. [2]

You don't have to be part of this percentage. If you are inactive, here's an easy way to begin adding activity into your life. A recent study stated that walking for 5 minutes at a time, 6 times per day, on most days of the week can improve heart health.[5]

Cancer is the second leading cause of death among Americans.

Walking can reduce the risk of some cancers by 50%. [6]

Stroke is the third leading cause of death; high blood pressure is a major risk factor for strokes.

Physical activity such as walking can not only prevent and reduce the high blood pressure that leads to strokes; it can also prevent the strokes as well.[7]

High cholesterol is a risk factor for strokes, heart disease and heart attacks.

One study showed that walking could improve cholesterol ratios and reduce heart disease risk whether one walked fast or slow.[8]

Other benefits of walking include the prevention and control of diabetes.[6,9] Walking is also an effective means of weight loss as it helps shed fat while keeping muscle. Muscle is good because it actually helps burn calories. Walking is also one of the most effective methods for maintaining weight loss over time.

Walking helps prevent and reduce debilitating problems such as back pain and osteoporosis. Brisk walking has also been shown to strengthen the immune system and help fight stress, potentially preventing colds and flu. [9]

The 'Golden Standard' for maximizing the physical benefits derived from exercise is 30 minutes or more of activity, most days of the week. The 30 minutes should be performed at a pace faster than a stroll, but slow enough to engage in conversation. The bottom line: physical activity is important and does have beneficial effects even if you aren't able to achieve the 'Golden Standard' right away. Start slowly, be comfortable and choose something fun!

The benefits obtained from walking are transferable to hiking. Hiking is considered to be more vigorous than walking, even when traveling at the same speed. This is due to probable trail surface conditions such as rocks, roots, gravel and varying terrain.

Psychological Benefits of Walking/Hiking

Many people are unaware that the simple act of walking or hiking can provide a multitude of psychological benefits beyond the expected physical ones. It has been shown that:

- Exercise is linked to a reduction of stress

- Exercise can be used for prevention and treatment of mild to moderate depression

- Exercise is associated with reductions in anxiety disorders

- Exercise has beneficial emotional effects across all ages and in both sexes

- Exercise improves physical fitness, which can lead to better mental health, increased self esteem and greater feelings of well-being. [10]

There's more! Here are some quick takes from professional studies.

Newer research reveals that exercise can help the cognitive functioning of the brain. In other words, people are able to think better because they exercise. [11] Other research showed that walking reduced the risk of memory loss or the decline of mental functioning as people become older. Their recommendation: walk a mile or more per day. [12] All ages can benefit from exercise. [13]

Studies demonstrate that exercise can reduce cravings for high fat or high sugar snack foods. [14] It can also decrease appetite for some people. [14]

Exercise has been shown to reduce cravings for smoking. [14]

Forget the caffeine...exercise increases energy levels for several hours afterward. [14]

So get smart! During work breaks, instead of grabbing a high fat/sugar snack, cigarette or caffeinated beverage, grab a short, brisk walk instead. It satisfies.

Hiking outdoors produces many benefits for mental health that go beyond the effects of the exercise itself. Simply being in the outdoors adds a sense of calm and peace. Just looking at the color green has been shown to have such a calming effect that classroom "blackboards" across the country were changed to green in order to have a soothing effect on students.

Social Benefits of Walking/Hiking

Many therapists utilize outdoor pursuits to effect changes in interpersonal relationships. Hiking may be more of a social activity than walking. Most people take along at least one other person when venturing out for a hike for safety as well as other reasons. Additionally, people often want to share the special beauty, sights and sounds of the outdoors with someone. There are no TVs blaring, no phones ringing (leave the cell phone off!), no chores calling while outside. New terrain to explore and discuss gives additional advantage to hiking. Couples and friends can improve their relationships by talking while walking. In one study, couples found themselves growing closer because of the additional time spent together without competing distractions.[15]

So, grab a friend and/or loved one to share a trail with you. But please remember that others on the trail may be seeking solitude or a spiritual experience. Therefore, remember to keep conversation volume down as voices travel a long way in the woods, especially near water.

Spiritual Benefits of Walking/Hiking

There is no question that being out in nature can awaken a deep part of us like nothing else can. For many people, walking in the woods or other natural settings can help them to realize or access feelings of spirituality in ways not possible through other methods. A recent article found that people often use such recreational activities as camping, canoeing, walking or riding in wooded areas, and even gardening to connect to their inner spirituality.[16] It seems that natural environments serve as a type of connection to spiritual experience. Since time is at such a premium in most people's lives, it has been suggested to use exercise time (walking, running, hiking, etc.) to commune with God or to pray.[17] Many people feel an enormous sense of peace or an enlarging of the soul where time seems to slow down, and problems seem to drift away.

It is the authors' hope that all of this information will encourage you to get out there and start hiking!

Don't wait to hike, even if you can't get to the North Shore area. Explore local trails where you live. Start a walking/hiking club in your own neighborhood.

Read other reputable health and fitness books (see Appendix A for suggestions).

Remember that the healthy lifestyle you create today can then take you to the North Shore and beyond tomorrow....

Wishing you a lifetime of healthy trails—however you travel them.

Note: The information presented herein is in NO way intended to substitute for medical advice. It is best to seek medical advice from a reputable medical professional. For your maximum well-being, we strongly recommend getting your doctor's approval before beginning a physical activity program.

FOR TRAVELERS WITH SPECIFIC NEEDS

FOR OUR READERS WITH PHYSICAL CHALLENGES

This chapter summarizes some of the information included throughout this book that may be of assistance to our readers with physical challenges. For a full description of each trail, Almost Hike, wayside or picnic area, please see their respective sections.

A Tribute

Throughout the course of writing this book we have come to realize something so powerful that no earthly force can dampen it. On the trails, we have often encountered face to face the immeasurable power of the human spirit in people with braces, wheelchairs, crutches, physical weaknesses, amputations and more.

Deeply moved by one person's tenacity of spirit, we wanted to share his story. His name is Paul Hlina. In 1995, he was the first documented through-hiker of the Superior Hiking Trail. We found this to be an impressive accomplishment in and of itself, but there's more. Paul hiked the entire 200 miles of this trail on crutches due to his paralyzed lower extremities.[1]

A Candid Message

After hearing the true story of a man who took his wife (in a wheelchair) on a trail that contained over 300 steps (encountered throughout) and inclines at 36% grade—we had to pause and reflect on what we say regarding accessibility. While we are hesitant to label hikes as accessible or not, we do aspire to present the trails in our book with honesty, integrity and straightforwardness. As we reviewed the Regulatory Negotiation Committee on Accessibility Guidelines for Outdoor Developed Areas (Final Report, September 30, 1999), we knew we were not qualified to assess our trails according to these standards, nor have we attempted to do so.

Given the geography of the North Shore, which is known for its rugged cliffs and terrain, we put much effort into finding the gentlest trails. With that said, many of our trails—even though considered gentle (see pg. 18 for our rating criteria)—fall outside of the parameters of the proposed accessibility guidelines. Although a few of our trails may meet Universal Design Standards, we only indicate those that the state parks claim as officially meeting such standards.

The Trails

Trails that meet the standards for Universal Design (as stated by their respective State Park) are: Gooseberry Falls (pg. 56), Plaza Overlook Loop (pg. 58) and High Falls at Grand Portage (pg. 128). All three of these trails made our best waterfall list as well. See our Authors' Corner on pg. 13, which lists other categories such as Best Lake Superior Views, Best River Views, etc.

On all other trails in this book, we note those things that may present challenges (e.g., inclines, rocks, roots, steps, etc.) as well as those features that may be helpful (e.g., benches, handrailings, paved trails, etc.). On each trail we state total trail length, trail surface, average tread width, total number of inclines and the steepest and longest (exceeding 30') incline. We report all inclines exceeding 10 degrees (18% grade). We used a clinometer to measure the inclines (running slope, not cross-slope) and chose to report in degrees rather than % grade (see Appendix C for conversion chart).

We put significant detail on each trail so our readers would know the locations (rounded to tenths of a mile) of various features. This way each person could make an informed decision based on his/her abilities as to how far to go on a certain trail or whether to choose another altogether.

Inclines on the Trails

On all of our trails, we report inclines. If a trail has no inclines greater than 10 degrees (18% grade), it does not necessarily mean that it is flat. The trail could (and often does) have inclines of lesser degrees. To alert our readers to the flattest trails (flattest defined by what our naked eye could perceive), we formed a list also displayed in Authors' Corner, but repeated here for your convenience.

Flattest Trails

Bayfront Festival Park 22
Lakewalk—from canal wall to Bayfront Festival Park 25
Lakewalk—from canal wall to Fitgers 26
Lester Park Trail (with a few exceptions; see below) 48
Knife River (with a few exceptions; see below) 50
Gooseberry River Loop 64
Little Two Harbors Paved Trail 66
Brule River Loop 122
Webster-Ashburton Trail & Picnic Area (with a few exceptions; see below) .126
High Falls at Grand Portage 128

Lester Park Trail has a few very short dips. Knife River is the flattest section of the Superior Hiking Trail that we could find, but has a few very short dips as well. It also has small areas that may retain water after heavy rain, and there are no footbridges. Currently, Knife River is the very beginning of the magnificent 235-mile Superior Hiking Trail. Gooseberry River Loop is paved for the first 0.2 miles (shares Gooseberry Falls trail), but has some root and rock immediately after the Upper Falls view. The second half of the trail is primarily boardwalk. The Little Two Harbors Paved Trail may have cracks in the asphalt and small bumps. Brule River Loop has one set of steps (17, wood, handrail). The Webster-Ashburton Trail & Picnic Area is paves for most of the way, but spur trails to picnic tables are not paved, nor is the path to the historical marker. For a complete listing of all paved trails and shortest trails, refer to the Authors' Corner on pg. 13.

Almost Hikes

These represent some of the shortest hikes in our book and deliver great views! Most are under 0.5 mile in total length. We list below the paved and flattest Almost Hikes that we could find. However, we highly recommend reading the individual descriptions (beginning on pg. 130) as these Almost Hikes vary in trail surface and terrain. None have been classified as meeting Universal Design Standards.

Paved and flattest (with the exception of access ramps)

If we were to classify these in Authors' Corner, both would receive Best Lake Superior Views listings! Although not a category, Canal Park Lighthouse Stroll would take Best for Viewing Ships—hands down.

Other Almost Hike possibilities for wheelchair accessibility (purely subjective)

Waysides, Scenic Locales and Picnic Areas

We created charts in order to feature those areas that have one or more accessible features. To assist those who need specific information on wheelchair accessibility, we indicate designated parking spaces and other facts that may be helpful. Since this chart is not a comprehensive listing of all the waysides, scenic locales and picnic areas in this book, please refer to their individual descriptions.

Note: Although not listed on the charts, Good Harbor Bay Wayside (pg. 155) and Pincushion Mountain Overlook (pg. 156) have wheelchair accessible informational markers.

These waysides and scenic locales have one or more accessible features.

WAYSIDE/SCENIC LOCALE	PAGE NUMBER	RESTROOM TYPE	RESTROOM ACCESSIBLE	SURFACE TO RESTROOM	SURFACE TO TABLES	SURFACE UNDER TABLE	TABLE EXTENSION	DESIGNATED PARKING	VIEWS FROM CAR	VISITOR CENTER
French River Hatchery	147	Portable		Paved				X	X	
Knife River	148	Vault	X	Paved	Paved	Paved		X		
Flood Bay	150	Vault	X	Paved				X	X	
Split Rock	152								X	
Cross River	154	Vault	X	Paved				X		
Cutface Creek Rest Area	155	Vault	X	Paved	Paved & grass	Paved		X		
Pincushion Mtn	156	Vault	X	Paved					X	
Grand Marais Public Water Access	156	Portable		Gravel	Grass & gravel	Grass & gravel	X	X	X	
Kadunce River	158				Paved	Paved		X	X	
Grand Portage Bay Rest Area	159	Flush	X	Paved	Paved	Paved		X	X	X
Isle Royale & Suzie Islands Overlook #1	159	Vault	X	Paved	Paved				X	

These picnic areas have one or more accessible features.

PICNIC AREA	PAGE NUMBER	SURFACE TO TABLES	SURFACE UNDER TABLE	TABLE EXTENSION	RESTROOM TYPE	RESTROOM ACCESSIBLE	SURFACE TO RESTROOM	DESIGNATED PARKING
Lakeview Park	164	Grass	Paved, grass		Flush	X	Grass	
Gooseberry Falls	166	Grass	Paved, grass		Flush	X	Grass	
Pebble Beach	166	Grass, dirt gravel	Grass, dirt gravel		Vault	X	Paved	X
Trail Center/Lakeview	167	Paved	Paved		Flush	X	Paved	X
Bayside Park	168	Gravel	Gravel	X	Vault		Dirt, gravel	X
Tettegouche General	168	Paved	Paved, grass		Flush	X	Paved	X
Bensen Lake	170	Grass	Grass		Vault	X	Dirt	
Temperance River	171	Grass, dirt gravel	Grass, dirt gravel		Vault	X	Dirt	
Grand Marais Recreational Area	172	Gravel	Paved	X	Portable		Gravel	
Grand Portage Monument	173	Grass, dirt	Grass, dirt		Flush	X	Grass, dirt	X

When Snowflakes Fly

The only paved trail plowed during snow season is Duluth's entire Lakewalk, however, access ramps may be iced over and patches of ice are likely on the trail. If using the Lakewalk in winter, we recommend calling ahead for conditions (Duluth Parks and Recreation, Maintenance: (218) 723-3425). Also, many of the waysides are closed during snow season as they are not plowed.

RESOURCES
Wilderness Inquiry (WI)

808 14th Avenue SE
Minneapolis, MN 55414
612.676.9400 or 1.800.728.0719
Fax 612.676.9401; email info@wildernessinquiry.org

"Wilderness Inquiry provides outdoor adventure for people of all ages, abilities, and backgrounds. WI travels to over 35 destinations by canoe, sea kayak, dog sled, horse pack, and back pack. Join the community of Wilderness Inquirers. All you need is a sense of adventure." www.wildernessinquiry.org

Department of Natural Resources (DNR)

500 Lafayette Road
St. Paul, MN 55155-4040
(651) 296-6157 or 1-888-646-6367

Through its 'Open the Outdoors' program, "the DNR provides a range of outdoor recreational opportunities, licenses, and permits for people with disabilities." www.dnr.state.mn.us

Access Outdoors

"Access Outdoors' website is an information resource for persons with disabilities who are looking for trips, destinations, products and services related to accessible outdoor recreation." www.accessoutdoors.org

REFERENCES
1. Slade, A. (Ed.) (2001). Guide to the Superior Hiking Trail. Two Harbors, MN: Ridgeline Press. pg. 2.

Welcome to Minnesota's North Shore and the 'All-American' Scenic Byway—Highway 61!

The North Shore Scenic Drive originates in Duluth and continues 150 miles to the Canadian border. Allow plenty of time as this road is not only scenic and beautiful, but is also a two lane highway (occasional passing lanes) with frequent curves and deer crossings.

This chapter summarizes some of the information included throughout this book regarding state parks, trails, Almost Hikes, waysides and picnic areas that may be of assistance to our readers traveling in RVs. For a full description of each of the trails, Almost Hikes, wayside and picnic areas, please see their respective chapters.

State Parks

The following state parks have entire lots designed for RV parking:

Gooseberry Falls State Park and Tettegouche State Park.

The following have designated RV parking spaces within a lot shared with other vehicles: Tettegouche State Park (High Falls picnic area), Split Rock Lighthouse State Park.

Trails

Parking areas for the following trails have designated RV spaces:

Almost Hikes

Parking areas for the following Almost Hikes have designated RV spaces:

Waysides and Scenic Locales

During the course of writing this book we visited every wayside and scenic locale so we could showcase the most scenic terrain that the North Shore has to offer. We think that you'll be delighted with our selections.

To help you plan ahead, we list only those that have designated RV parking or highway pull-throughs (plus we tell you other information at a glance that may be helpful). We list them in chart format for your convenience and state the following information: Designated parking, highway pull-through, type of restroom, picnic tables and visitor center.

Designated parking: Indicates that there are spaces specifically designed to accommodate RVs.

Highway pull-through: A designated area with an easy exit off the highway and an easy entrance back onto the highway. Since there are no designated parking places, RV access and pull-through capabilities will be determined by how vehicles are positioned.

Type of restroom: Indicates toilet type—flush (modern), vault (pit), portable (port-a-pottys, portalets).

Picnic tables: We included the nicest ones, but do check out our 'spread' on picnic areas (pg. 162-174).

Visitor center: Indicates if there is a center at the site or nearby.

Please note: Palisade Head Overlook does not allow trailers due to its very narrow and winding road construction. RV travel is not recommended either.

Also, many of the waysides are closed during snow season as they are not plowed.

Picnic Areas

During the course of writing this book we visited every picnic area so we could choose the very best that the North Shore has to offer.

We list only the picnic areas below that have designated RV parking, but we encourage you to read through our detailed descriptions of the rest of the picnic areas in starting on pg. 162.

Picnic areas with designated RV parking

Cascade River Picnic Area (pg. 172) is accessed via a pull-through road off Highway 61 that has no designed parking spaces for anyone, but allows parking on the side of that road.

*Bayside Park (pg. 168) caters to RVs quite nicely; however, there are certain areas in the park (a picnic area included) that do not permit trailer or RV access due to the narrow and winding roads.

These as well as all picnic areas featured in this book have a knack for working up an appetite for scenic beauty. Bon appetit!

These waysides and scenic locales have features useful for those traveling in RVs.

WAYSIDE/SCENIC LOCALE	PAGE NUMBER	DESIGNATED RV PARKING	HWY PULL-THROUGH	RESTROOM TYPE	PICNIC TABLES	VISITOR CENTER
Knife River	148	X		Vault	X	
Lighthouse Point Public Water Access	149	X		Portable	X	
Flood Bay	150	X		Vault		
Split Rock	152		X			
Cross River	154	X		Vault		
Cascade River	154		X			
Good Harbor Bay	155		X			
Cutface Creek Rest Area	155	X		Vault	X	
Grand Marais Public Water Access	156	X		Portable	X	Nearby
Grand Portage Bay Rest Area	159	X		Flush	X	X
Isle Royale & Suzie Islands Overlook #1	159	X		Vault	X	
Isle Royale & Suzie Islands Overlook #2	160		X			

APPENDICES

APPENDIX A: RECOMMENDED READINGS AND RESOURCES

The following are recommended resources for your health and enjoyment.

Hiking

Fenton, H. *50 Circuit Hikes: a Stride-by-Stride Guide to Northeastern Minnesota*. Duluth, MN: Pfeifer-Hamilton Publishers, 1999.

Link, M. and K. Crowley. *Hiking Minnesota*. Champaign, IL: Human Kinetics, 1999.

McGrath, W. C. *Great Minnesota Walks: 49 Strolls, Rambles, Hikes, and Treks*. Madison, WI: Trails Books, 1999.

Pukite, J. *Hiking Minnesota*. Helena, MT: Falcon Publishing Co., Inc., 1998.

Slade, A. (Ed.) *Guide to the Superior Hiking Trail*. Two Harbors, MN: Ridgeline Press, 2001.

State Parks

Arthur, A. *Minnesota's State Parks*. Cambridge, MN: Adventure Publications, Inc., 1998.

History

Aubut, S.T. and M.C. Norton. *Images of America: Duluth Minnesota*. Chicago: Arcadia Publishing, 2001.

Young, F. A. *Duluth's Ship Canal and Aerial Bridge: How They Came to Be*. Duluth, MN: Stewart-Taylor Company, 1977.

Biking

Mickelson, M. *Biking in Vikingland*. Cambridge, MN: Adventure Publications, Inc., 1999.

Richardson, S. *Biking Wisconsin's Rail-Trails*. Cambridge, MN: Adventure Publications, Inc., 1997.

Cross-country Skiing

Slade, A. *White Woods, Quiet Trails: Exploring Minnesota's North Shore in Winter*. Two Harbors, MN: Ridgeline Press, 1997.

Field Guides

McCarthy, A. *Critters of Minnesota Pocket Guide*. Cambridge, MN: Adventure Publications, Inc., 2000.

Tekiela, S. *Birds of Minnesota Field Guide*. Cambridge, MN: Adventure Publications, Inc., 1998.

Tekiela, S. *Birds of Prey of Minnesota Field Guide*. Cambridge, MN: Adventure Publications, Inc., 2002.

Tekiela, S. *Wildflowers of Minnesota Field Guide*. Cambridge, MN: Adventure Publications, Inc., 1999.

Tekiela, S. *Trees of Minnesota Field Guide*. Cambridge, MN: Adventure Publications, Inc., 2001.

Tekiela, S. *Birds of Wisconsin Field Guide*. Cambridge, MN: Adventure Publications, Inc., 1999.

Tekiela, S. *Wildflowers of Wisconsin Field Guide*. Cambridge, MN: Adventure Publications, Inc., 2000.

Tekiela, S. *Trees of Wisconsin Field Guide*. Cambridge, MN: Adventure Publications, Inc., 2002.

North Shore

Hereid, N. and E.D. Gennaro. *A Family Guide to Minnesota's North Shore*. Minneapolis: Minnesota Sea Grant, 1993.

Perich, S. *The North Shore: a Four-season Guide to Minnesota's Favorite Destination*. Duluth, MN: Pfeifer-Hamilton, 1992.

Simonowicz, N. A. *Nina's North Shore Guide*. Minneapolis: University of Minnesota Press, 1999.

Health and Wellness

Alsbro, D. *The Best Little Book of Wellness*. Benton Harbor, MI: Rainbow Wellness, 2000.

Cooper, K. *Faith-Based Fitness*. Nashville, TN: Thomas Nelson Publishers, 1997.

Leith, L.M. *Exercising Your Way to Better Mental Health*. Morgantown, WV: Fitness Information Technology, 1998.

Walking

Sweetgall, R. *Walk the Four Seasons: Walking and Cross-training Logbook*. Clayton, MO: Creative Walking, Inc., 1992.

Stretching

Anderson, B. and J. Anderson. *Stretching (Revised)*. Berkeley, CA: Publishers Group West, 2000.

Additional Resources, Including Websites

For access to all the links in the appendices and additional links about health and the North Shore, visit http://www.d.umn.edu/~ltornabe/gh.

Department of Natural Resources
500 Lafayette Road
St. Paul, MN 55155-4040
651-296-6157 (Metro Area)
1-800-646-6367 or www.dnr.state.mn.us

Superior Hiking Trail Association (SHTA)
P.O. Box 4
Two Harbors, MN 55616-0004
(218) 834-2700, www.shta.org or suphike@mr.net

Wilderness Inquiry (WI)
"Wilderness Inquiry provides outdoor adventure for people of all ages, abilities, and backgrounds. WI travels to over 35 destinations by canoe, sea kayak, dog sled, horse pack, and back pack. Join the community of Wilderness Inquirers. All you need is a sense of adventure." www.wildernessinquiry.org

Access Outdoors
"Access Outdoors' website is an information resource for persons with disabilities who are looking for trips, destinations, products and services related to accessible outdoor recreation." www.accessoutdoors.org

Vacation Planning (chronological order)

Duluth Convention and Business Bureau
1-800-438-5884 or www.visitduluth.com
North Shore Scenic Drive Association
www.northshorescenicdrive.com

Two Harbors Area Chamber of Commerce
1-800-777-7384 or (218) 834-2600 or www.twoharbors.com/chamber
chamber@twoharbors.com

Lake County R.J. Houle Visitor Center
On Highway 61 just outside of town in Two Harbors
1-800-554-2116 or www.lakecnty.com

Lutsen-Tofte Tourism Association
1-888-61NORTH or www.61north.com

Silver Bay/Beaver Bay Area Chamber of Commerce
(218) 226-4870

Silver Bay information center (seasonal) and city website
(218) 226-3143, www.silverbay.com

Grand Marais Area Chamber of Commerce
(218) 387-1400 or www.grandmarais.com

Grand Portage National Monument Great Hall Visitor Center
(218) 475-2202

Book Credits

Superior Calls (poem, pg. 199)
Written especially for 'Gentle Hikes' by peeje.
"Thoughts by peeje" is a collection of poetry featuring the North Shore and Lake Superior. For more information, contact peeje1@juno.com

APPENDIX B: TRAIL HEADQUARTERS INFORMATION

The following is a list of phone numbers, addresses and applicable websites of all trail headquarters pertaining to the trails featured in this book.

A common phone number and website for all MN state parks is the Department of Natural Resources (1-888-646-6367, www.dnr.state.mn.us), but for specific information, contact the individual parks.

Cascade River State Park
3481 West Highway 61
Lutsen, MN 55612-9535
(218) 387-3053

George H. Crosby Manitou State Park
Send mail c/o Tettegouche State Park
5702 Highway 61
Silver Bay, MN 55614-4215
(218) 226-6365

Gooseberry Falls State Park
3206 Highway 61
Two Harbors, MN 55616-2010
(218) 834-3855
(218) 834-3787 (fax)

Grand Portage State Park
9393 East Highway 61
Grand Portage, Minnesota 55605-3000
(218) 475-2360

Judge C.R. Magney State Park
4051 East Highway 61
Grand Marais, Minnesota 55604-2150
(218) 387-3039

Split Rock Lighthouse State Park
3755 Split Rock Lighthouse Road
Two Harbors, MN 55616-2020
(218) 226-6377

Temperance River State Park
Box 33
Schroeder, MN 55613-0033
(218) 663-7476

Tettegouche State Park
5702 Highway 61
Silver Bay, Minnesota 55614-4215
(218) 226-6365

Duluth Parks and Recreation
Department of Maintenance
12 E 4th Street
Duluth, MN 55805
(218) 723-3425

Pincushion Mountain Bed & Breakfast
968 Gunflint Trail
Grand Marais, MN 55604
(218) 387-1276 or www.pincushionbb.com

Sugarloaf Interpretive Center Association
244 Marks Road
Esko, MN 55733
(218) 879-4334
email: SUGARLOAFINT@msn.com

Superior Hiking Trail Association (SHTA)*
P.O. Box 4
Two Harbors, MN 55616-0004
(218) 834-2700 or www.shta.org
email: suphike@mr.net

*If you are visiting Two Harbors and wish to drop by the SHTA office/store, it is located two blocks west of Dairy Queen at 731 Seventh Avenue (downstairs).

Silver Bay information center (seasonal)
(218) 226-3143

Grand Marais Area Chamber of Commerce
13 N Broadway
Grand Marais, MN 55604
(218) 387-1400 or www.grandmarais.com

Two Harbors Area Chamber of Commerce
1-800-777-7384 or (218) 834-2600 or www.twoharbors.com/chamber
email: chamber@twoharbors.com

Forgive us, but remember that two of us are professors and the other—a former accountant!

Measuring distances

All trails were rolled with a Rolotape (400 series—professional). Distances were recorded in feet, then rounded to the nearest tenth of a mile.

Measuring inclines

Inclines were measured with a clinometer (Suunto MC-2G Global Navigator).

Inclines were reported on an average of various places on the slope.

All were reported in this book in degrees. The following is a conversion chart for those desiring the same information reported in % grade.

Conversion of degrees to % grade
10 degrees is 18% grade
12 degrees is 21% grade
14 degrees is 25% grade
16 degrees is 29% grade
18 degrees is 32% grade
20 degrees is 36% grade
22 degrees is 40% grade

Formula: To convert degrees to % grade, use a calculator with a tangent function. Enter the number of degrees, then press the 'tan' button. For an approximation, double the degrees and the answer will be close to the % grade.

Trail hiking time frame

All trails in this book were hiked by at least two of the authors in the summer of 2001. We hiked again to ensure accuracy in the Fall of 2001. Conditions were reported as accurately as possible; however, conditions can change due to environmental factors. Improvements continue to be made on trails.

We advise you to call ahead to the respective trail headquarters for current conditions (phone numbers are provided after 'Trailhead Directions' on all hiking trails; the Superior Hiking Trail Association also posts conditions on their website at www.shta.org).

Photography credits

All photos were taken by the authors with a Cannon AE-1 35mm camera using a variety of slide film ranging from amateur to professional.

References used in writing this book

Aubut, S.T. and M.C. Norton. *Images of America: Duluth, Minnesota.* Chicago: Arcadia Publishing, 2001.

Duluth Convention and Visitors Bureau. *Your Free Guide to Simple Pleasures* [Booklet], 2001.

Slade, A. (Ed.) *Guide to the Superior Hiking Trail.* Two Harbors, MN: Ridgeline Press, 2001.

National Scenic Byways Program
http://www.byways.org/travel/scenicbyways.html

References for Hiking for Health and Says Who ...

1. D. Schardt, "These Feet Were Made for Walking: Health Benefits of Walking and Other Moderate Exercise," *Nutrition Action Healthletter* 20, no.10 (Dec1993):4. **2.** J E Manson, F.B. Hu, J.W. Rich-Edwards and others, "A Prospective Study of Walking as Compared with Vigorous Exercise in the Prevention of Coronary Heart Disease in Women," *New England Journal of Medicine* 341, no. 9 (Aug 26 1999):650–658. **3.** A.A. Hakim, J.D. Curb, H. Petrovitch and others, "Effects of Walking on Coronary Heart Disease in Elderly Men: The Honolulu Heart Program," *Circulation* 100, no. 1 (Jul 6 1999): 9–13. **4.** K.E. Powell, K.D. Thompson, C.J. Casperson, J.S. Kendrick, "Physical Activity and the Incidence of Coronary Artery Disease," *Annual Review of Public Health* 8 (1987): 253–287. **5.** K.J. Coleman, H.R. Raynor, D.M. Mueller and others, "Providing Sedentary Adults with Choices for Meeting Their Walking Goals," *Preventive Medicine* 28, no. 5 (1999): 510–519. **6.** "Physical Activity, Part II–Exercise: A Good Health Prescription," *Harvard Women's Health Watch* 8, no. 11 (Jul 2001):NA. **7.** F.B. Hu, M.J. Stampfer, G.A. Colditz and others, "Physical Activity and Risk of Stroke in Women," *Journal of the American Medical Association* 283, no. 2 (Jun 14 2000): 2961–67. **8.** J.J. Duncan, N.F. Gordon, C.B. Scott, "Women Walking for Health and Fitness: How Much is Enough?" *Journal of the American Medical Association* 266. no 23 (Dec 18 1991): 3295–99. **9.** S. Percy, "Putting One Foot in Front of the Other: Walking for Exercise," *Harvard Health Letter* 22, no. 6 (Apr 1997): 2. **10.** S.T. Walters, J.E. Martin, "Does Aerobic Exercise Really Enhance Self Esteem in Children? A Prospective Evaluation in 3rd–5th Graders," *Journal of Sport Behavior* 23, no.1 (Mar 2000):51–60. **11.** A.F. Kramer, N.J. Hahn, M.T. Banich and others, "Ageing, Fitness and Neurocognitive Function," *Nature* 400, no. 6743 (Jul 29 1999): 418–19. **12.** K. Yaffe, D. Barnes, M. Nevitt and others, "A Prospective Study of Physical Activity and Cognitive Decline in Elderly Women: Women Who Walk," *Archives of Internal Medicine* 161, no. 14 (Jul 23 2001): 1703–8. **13.** S. Brink, "Smart Moves: New Research Suggest that Folks from 8 to 80 Can Shape up Their Brains with Aerobic Exercise," *U.S. News & World Report* 118, no. 19 (May 15 1995) 76(6). **14.** R.E. Thayer, "Energy Walks: Don't Touch that Candy Bar. A Short Walk Gives You a Longer Energy Boost and Improves Your Mood," *Psychology Today* 22, no. 10 (Oct 1988): 12(2). **15.** D. Foltz-Gray, "Exercise in Romance: What's the Best Way to Renew Your Commitment to Fitness–and to Your Relationship? (Walking)" *Health* 15, no. 4 (May 2001): 48(3). **16.** J. McChesney, S. Knight, B. Boswell, M. Hamer, "Interrelatedness Between Recreational Activity and Spirituality: The Perspectives of Persons with Disabilities," *Research Quarterly for Exercise and Sport* 71, no. 1 (Mar 2000): Supplement: A-50. **17.** A. Bauman, "Running on Faith," *Runners World* 34, no. 6 (Jun 1999): 86 (1). **18.** S.G. Wannamethee, A.G. Shaper, M. Walker, "Physical Activity and Mortality in Older Men with Diagnosed Coronary Heart Disease," *Circulation* 102, no. 12

(Sep 19 2000): 1358–63. **19.** P. Seraganian, editor *Exercise Psychology: The Influence of Physical Exercise on Psychological Processes* (New York: John Wiley & Sons, 1993) **20.** L.M. Leith, *Foundations of Exercise and Mental Health* (Morgantown, WV: Fitness Information Technology, 1994) **21.** L.M. Leith, *Exercising Your Way to Better Mental Health* (Morgantown, WV: Fitness Information Technology, 1998) **22.** K.F. Hays, *Working It Out: Using Exercise in Psychotherapy* (Washington, DC: American Psychological Association, 1999) **23.** D.L. Drotar, "Reaching New Heights: Hiking Your Way to Physical and Mental Fitness," *American Fitness* 16, no. 3 (May–Jun 1998):48(3). **24.** M. Malecki, "Promoting Spiritual Wellness in Medical, Psychological and Other Health Care Settings: Assisting the Health Client to Access the Inner Healer," *Dissertation Abstracts International–Section B: The Sciences and Engineering* 56, no. 11-B (May 1996): 6030(190). **25.** M.J. Cohen, *Reconnecting with Nature* (Corvallis, OR: Ecopress, 1997) **26.** M.I. Wallace, "The Wild Bird Who Heals: Recovering the Spirit in Nature," *Theology Today* 50, no. 1 (Apr 1993): 13(16). **27.** G.A. Kelly, K.S. Kelly, Z.V. Tran, "Walking and Resting Blood Pressure in Adults: A Meta-Analysis," *Preventive Medicine* 33 (2001): 120–127. **28.** "Hitting the Trail in Good Form," *Harvard Women's Health Letter* 7, no. 10 (June 2000): NA **29.** D.H. Passe, M. Horn, R. Murray, "Impact of Beverage Acceptability on Fluid Intake During Exercise," *Appetite* 35 (2000): 219–229. **30.** F. Sizer, E. Whitney, *Nutrition: Concepts and Controversies (8th edition)* (Belmont, CA: Wadsworth)

SUPERIOR CALLS

Come home to my shores, where your soul longs to be
Bring your worries and cares, spend time with me

Rest from life in the shade of my birch
Daydream like a child as peace you search

Hear the laughter in my soul as waves crash my shore
Embrace the calm in your heart as you open the door

Feel contentment as my crystal waters refresh your soul
Hold tight to the passion that deep within you rolls

Walk my gentle trails and soon you'll begin to smile
Come to Superior and rest for awhile

peeje

(this poem was written as a tribute to this book)
copyright 2001

TRIBUTE TO SPLIT ROCK LIGHTHOUSE

Split Rock Lighthouse perched high
keeping watch, standing solid
guarding the shore

Your light will shine forever
commemorating the memory
you have engraved on so many souls.

written 8-14-01 by Ladona Tornabene

GLOSSARY OF TERMS:

This is not a conclusive list; however, we have included terms that may not be familiar to our readers that were used in our trails, Almost Hikes, waysides and picnic areas.

Amenities: Indicates availability of such things as restrooms, water fountains, visitor centers, picnic tables, playgrounds, grills, shelters, boat launches, etc. Note: For clarity, we indicate restrooms by toilet type: flush (modern), vault (pit), portable (port-a-pottys, portalets).

Boardwalk: Long boards laid side by side or end to end, to make walking easier over a particular section. These may be slippery when wet or frosted; may be loose in some areas; may be difficult to use with hiking poles or challenging to navigate if narrow. Always use caution when crossing them.

Laid log paths: Sometimes referred to as cut-log paths, these are normally laid side by side across the trail to facilitate crossing a muddy section, are often unsecured or loose. These may be challenging to navigate regardless of conditions. Always use caution when crossing them.

Seasonal: Many of our trailhead facilities and amenities will have a seasonal notation. Seasonal is typically defined as the period of time from mid-May to mid-October. This being Minnesota, these are close approximations based on ground freezing/thawing. Many of the waysides are closed during snow season as they are not plowed.

Spur Trail: A trail that connects to the main trail, typically leading to a point of interest or scenic overlook.

SHT: Abbreviation for the Superior Hiking Trail, a magnificent 235 mile footpath beginning in the town of Knife River and continuing to the Canadian border. We've selected the gentlest sections we could find to showcase in this book.

Universal Design Standards: Universal Design means that the trail meets accessibility standards for persons of all abilities.

Wheelchair accessible: We have used this term throughout the book regarding parking and other amenities. It is defined as a location that can be accessed by someone in a wheelchair. All flush toilets are wheelchair accessible unless otherwise noted; however, surfaces leading to flush toilets may not always be paved. Accessibility of vault toilets varies, but most have handrails. Surfaces leading to vault toilets are typically hardpacked dirt/gravel. None of the portable toilets we have seen meet the criteria for wheelchair accessibility.

CHECKLIST (USE THE BOXES TO CHECK THE TRAILS YOU'VE HIKED!)

TRAILS

Duluth to Two Harbors

- ☐ Bayfront Festival Park
- ☐ Lakewalk: Canal Wall to Bayfront Festival Park
- ☐ Lakewalk: Canal Wall to Fitgers
- ☐ Lakewalk: Rose Garden to Fitgers
- ☐ Lakewalk East: Rose Garden to Water Street
- ☐ Lakewalk East Extension: London Road to Water Street
- ☐ Bagley Nature Area–Rock Hill
- ☐ Bagley Nature Area: East Loop
- ☐ Bagley Nature Area: West Loop
- ☐ Congdon Park Trail
- ☐ Lester Park Trail
- ☐ Knife River
- ☐ Sonju Harbor Walking Trail: Lighthouse Loop
- ☐ Sonju Harbor Walking Trail: Burlington Bay to First Street

Beyond Two Harbors to Little Marais

- ☐ Gooseberry Falls (Gooseberry Falls State Park)
- ☐ Plaza Overlook Loop (Gooseberry Falls State Park)
- ☐ River View Trail (Gooseberry Falls State Park)
- ☐ Gitchi Gummi (Gooseberry Falls State Park)
- ☐ Gooseberry River Loop (Gooseberry Falls State Park)
- ☐ Little Two Harbors Paved Trail (Split Rock Lighthouse State Park)
- ☐ Little Two Harbors Trail (Split Rock Lighthouse State Park)
- ☐ Beaver River East
- ☐ North Shore Mining Scenic Overlook and Trails
- ☐ Triple Overlook Loop (Tettegouche State Park)
- ☐ Shovel Point Trail (Tettegouche State Park)
- ☐ Baptism River Loop (Tettegouche State Park)
- ☐ Fisherman's Trail (Tettegouche State Park)
- ☐ High Falls at Tettegouche (Tettegouche State Park)
- ☐ Tettegouche Lake Overlook (Tettegouche State Park)
- ☐ Bensen Lake Trail (George H. Crosby-Manitou State Park)

Beyond Little Marais to Grand Marais

- ☐ Sugarloaf Cove Trail
- ☐ Tower Overlook
- ☐ Temperance River Lower Loop (Temperance River State Park)
- ☐ Cauldron Trail (Temperance River State Park)
- ☐ Oberg Loop
- ☐ Poplar River Overlook
- ☐ Lower Cascade Falls Quick Route (Cascade River State Park)
- ☐ Lake Superior Shore (Cascade River State Park)
- ☐ Lower Falls Cascade River Loop (Cascade River State Park)
- ☐ Hidden Falls
- ☐ Overlook Snowshoe Trail
- ☐ Lighthouse Stroll

Beyond Grand Marais to Canadian Border

- ☐ Barrier Falls Overlook
- ☐ Kadunce River
- ☐ Brule River Loop (Judge C.R. Magney State Park)
- ☐ Gauthier Creek
- ☐ Webster–Ashburton Trail and Picnic Area (Grand Portage State Park)
- ☐ High Falls at Grand Portage (Grand Portage State Park)

ALMOST HIKES
Duluth to Two Harbors

- ☐ Canal Park Lighthouse Stroll
- ☐ Leif Erikson Rose Garden
- ☐ Rock Pond
- ☐ Two Rivers View
- ☐ Breakwater Lighthouse Point Stroll

Beyond Two Harbors to Little Marais

- ☐ Iona's Beach
- ☐ Pebble Beach (Split Rock Lighthouse State Park)
- ☐ Bayside Park

Beyond Little Marais to Grand Marais

- ☐ Father Baraga's Cross
- ☐ Temperance River Bridge View (Temperance River State Park)
- ☐ Best-kept Secret of Grand Marais
- ☐ Devil Track Wildflower Walk
- ☐ Artists' Point

WAYSIDES AND SCENIC LOCALES
Duluth to Two Harbors

- ☐ North Shore Visitor Center
- ☐ Scenic Highway 61
- ☐ French River Hatchery
- ☐ Buchanan Historical Marker
- ☐ Knife River Wayside
- ☐ Lighthouse Point Public Water Access

Beyond Two Harbors to Little Marais

- ☐ Flood Bay Wayside
- ☐ Stewart River Wayside
- ☐ Split Rock Wayside

Beyond Little Marais to Grand Marais

- ☐ Palisade Head Overlook
- ☐ Cross River Wayside
- ☐ Cascade River Wayside
- ☐ Good Harbor Wayside

- ☐ Cutface Creek Rest Area
- ☐ Pinchshion Mountain Overlook
- ☐ Grand Marais Public Water Access

Beyond Grand Marais to Canadian Border

- ☐ Kadunce River Wayside
- ☐ Old Dog Trail
- ☐ Grand Portage Bay Rest Area
- ☐ Isle Royale and Susie Islands Overlook #1
- ☐ Isle Royale and Susie Islands Overlook #2

PICNIC AREAS
Duluth to Two Harbors

- ☐ Kitchi Gammi Park
- ☐ Lakeview Park Picnic Area

Beyond Two Harbors to Little Marais

- ☐ Gooseberry Falls Picnic Areas (Gooseberry Falls State Park)
- ☐ Pebble Beach Picnic Area (Split Rock Lighthouse State Park)
- ☐ Trail Center/Lakeview Picnic Area (Split Rock Lighthouse State Park)
- ☐ Bayside Park Picnic Area
- ☐ Tettegouche General Picnic Areas (Tettegouche State Park)
- ☐ High Falls Picnic Area (Tettegouche State Park)
- ☐ Bensen Lake Picnic Area (George H. Crosby-Manitou State Park)

Beyond Little Marais to Grand Marais

- ☐ Father Baraga's Cross Picnic Area
- ☐ Temperance River Picnic Area (Temperance River State Park)
- ☐ Cascade River State Park Picnic Area (Cascade River State Park)
- ☐ Grand Marais Recreation Area

Beyond Grand Marais to Canadian Border

- ☐ Grand Portage National Monument Picnic Area
- ☐ Grand Portage State Park Picnic Area (Grand Portage State Park)

INDEX

ABOUT THE AUTHORS

From left to right, Ladona Tornabene, Champ (UMD's mascot), Melanie Morgan, Lisa Vogelsang

Trails of a "Champ"-ion

To support health education majors in pursuing their passion, Ladona Tornabene has started the Trails of a "Champ"-ion Scholarship Fund through the University of Minnesota Duluth. A portion of the proceeds from the sale of this book go to that scholarship fund.

About the Authors

Ladona Tornabene, Ph.D., CHES is an Assistant Professor of Health Education at the University of Minnesota Duluth. Her focus lies in confronting the number one public health problem in America today—lack of physical activity. This fact, combined with her sense of adventure and unquenchable appetite for scenic beauty, birthed a passion. That passion is to promote better health through opening the outdoors to people of all abilities. She believes that the North Shore, with its breathtaking scenery, is prime incentive for accomplishing such a mission. Though an advocate for active lifestyles, she desires for people to grasp that health is more than just being in good physical shape, it's psychological, social, environmental and spiritual as well. Her advice? For better inner health—Get out!

Melanie Morgan works at St. Mary's/Duluth Clinic in the medical field. Her knowledge of the North Shore and background in accounting and advertising have been instrumental to the completion of this book. As a Minnesota native, some of her fondest memories of family vacations are of traveling and camping along Minnesota's North Shore and up the Gunflint Trail. She developed an interest in the wonders of nature from her father, who shared his love of the outdoors with his children. Melanie and her husband, Mark, enjoy hiking and snowshoeing out the back door of their Duluth home. Some of her favorite activities include camping, canoeing, cross-country skiing, sewing, and quilting.

Lisa Vogelsang, Ph.D., is an Assistant Professor in Psychology at the University of Minnesota Duluth specializing in Health Psychology and Human Development. A former two-time Olympian, she loves the outdoors, especially Duluth and the North Shore area. Lisa enjoys hiking, biking, sea kayaking, cross country skiing and snowshoeing. After five ankle surgeries and developing severe arthritis from a previous athletic injury, she must keep her hikes short and less rugged. Her disability was, in part, a catalyst in the conception of this book.

All three authors are members of the Superior Hiking Trail Association and Friends of Minnesota State Parks.

For more Gentle Hikes pictures and information, visit the authors on the web at http://www.d.umn.edu/~ltornabe/gh